# CARIBBEAN

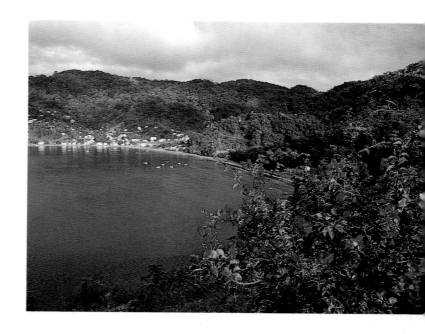

SMITHMARK

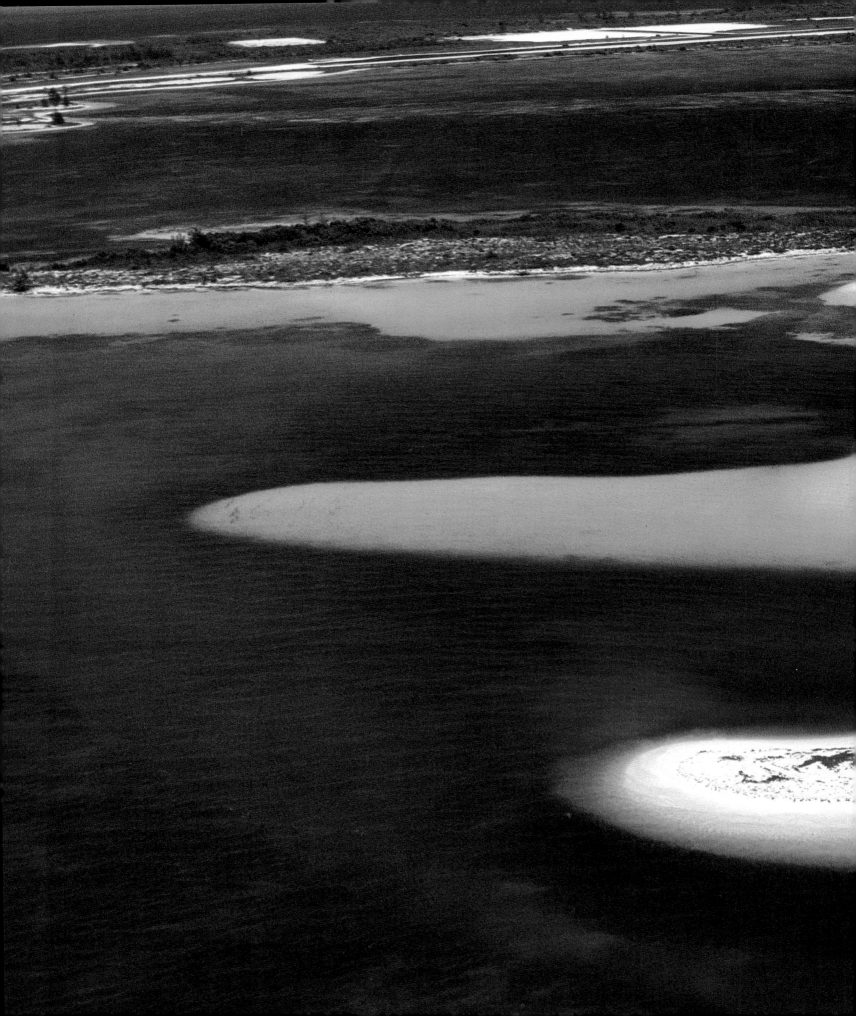

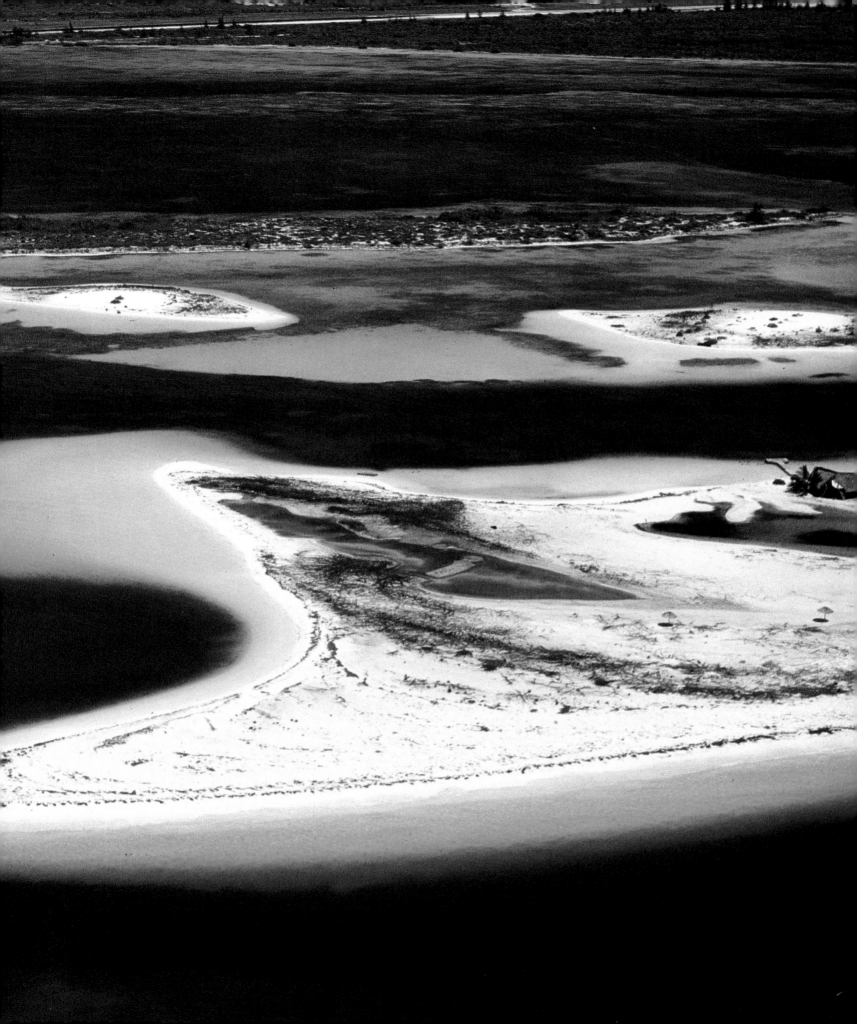

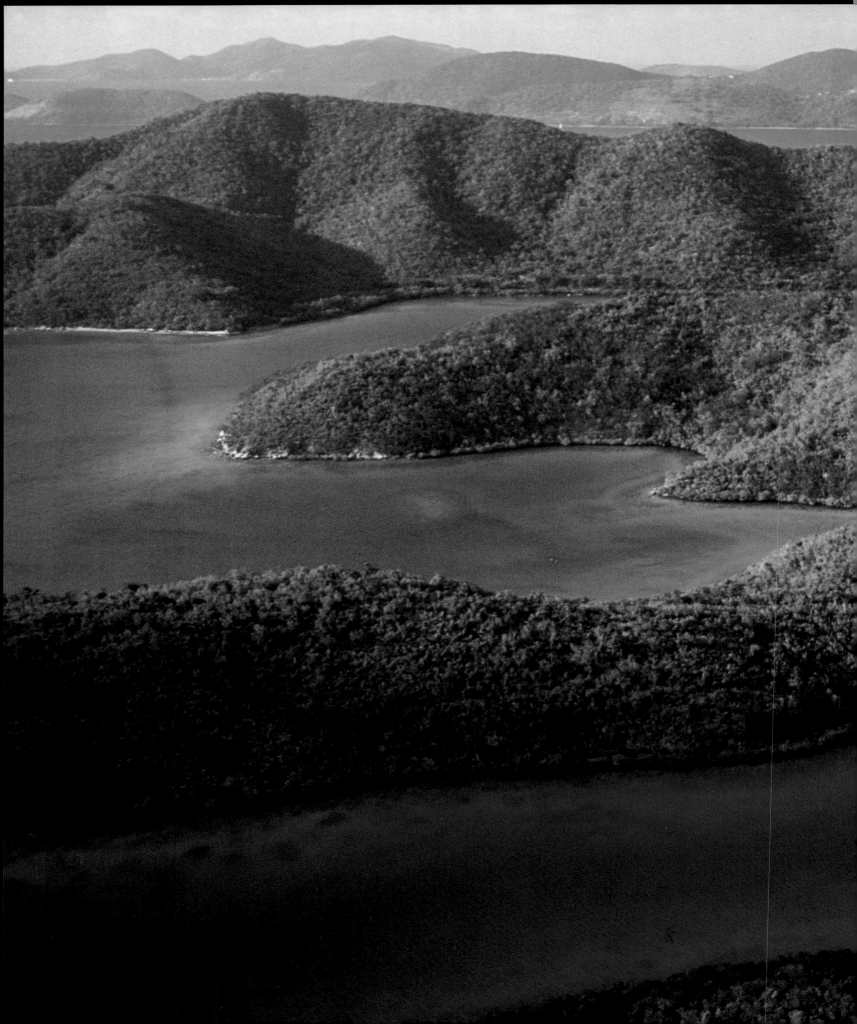

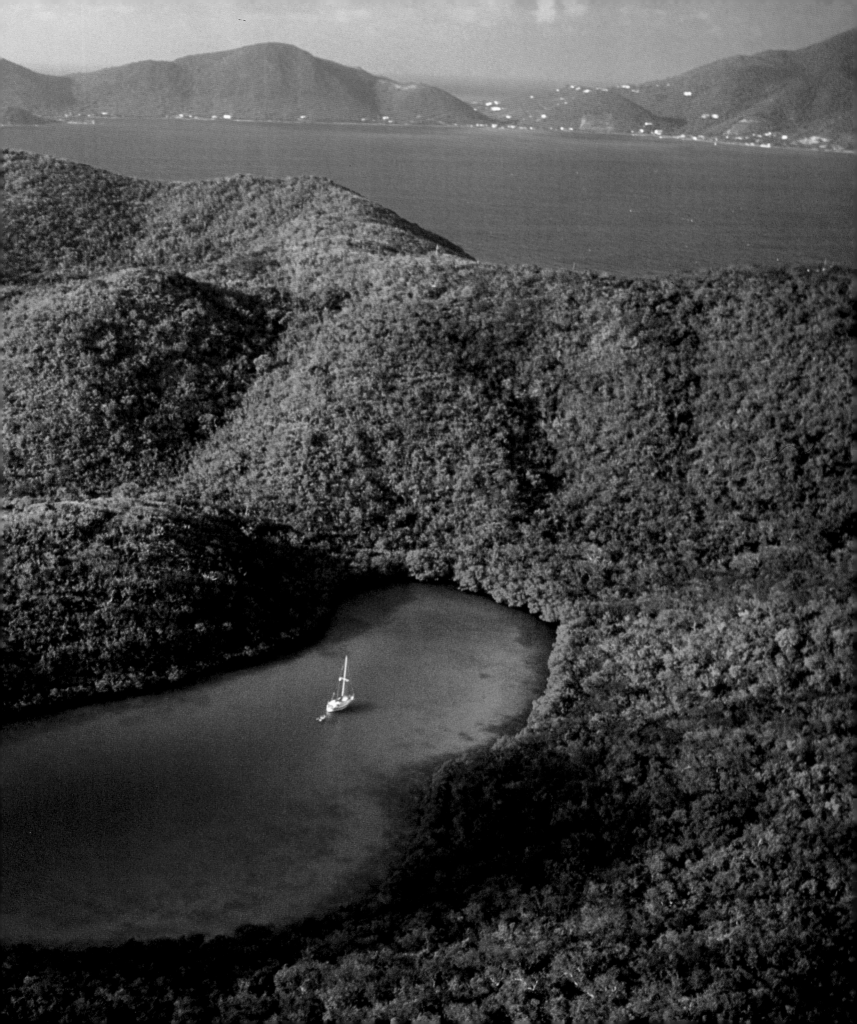

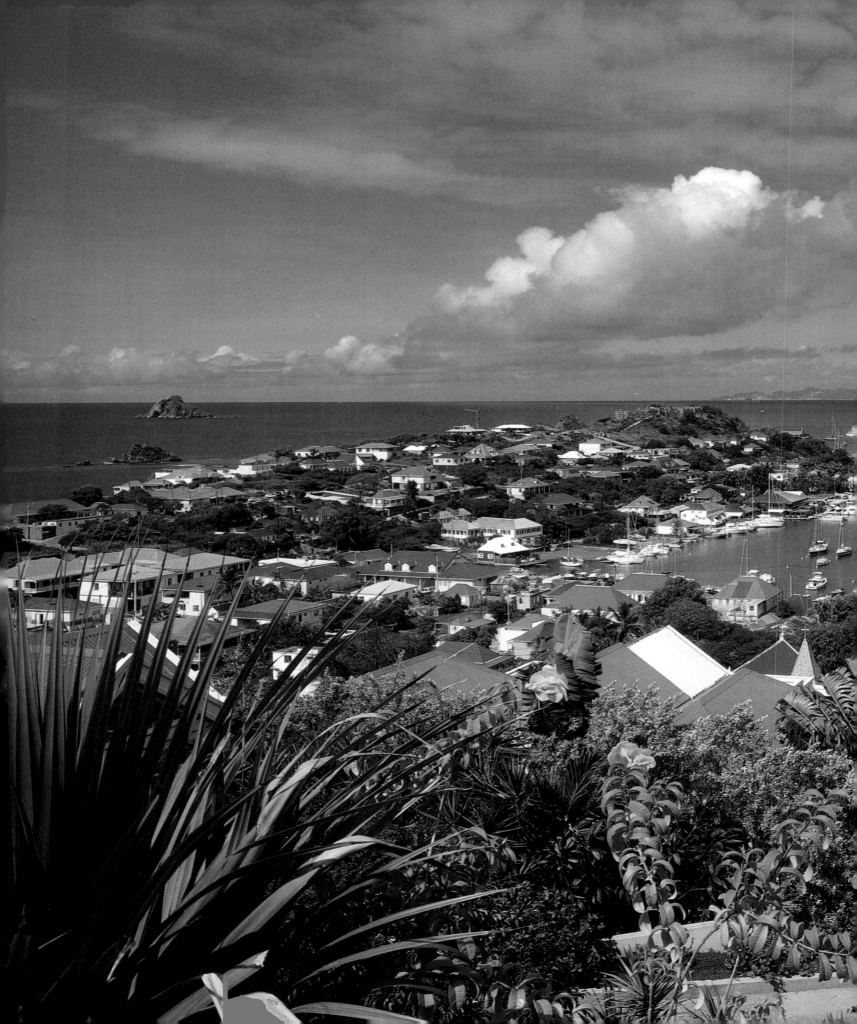

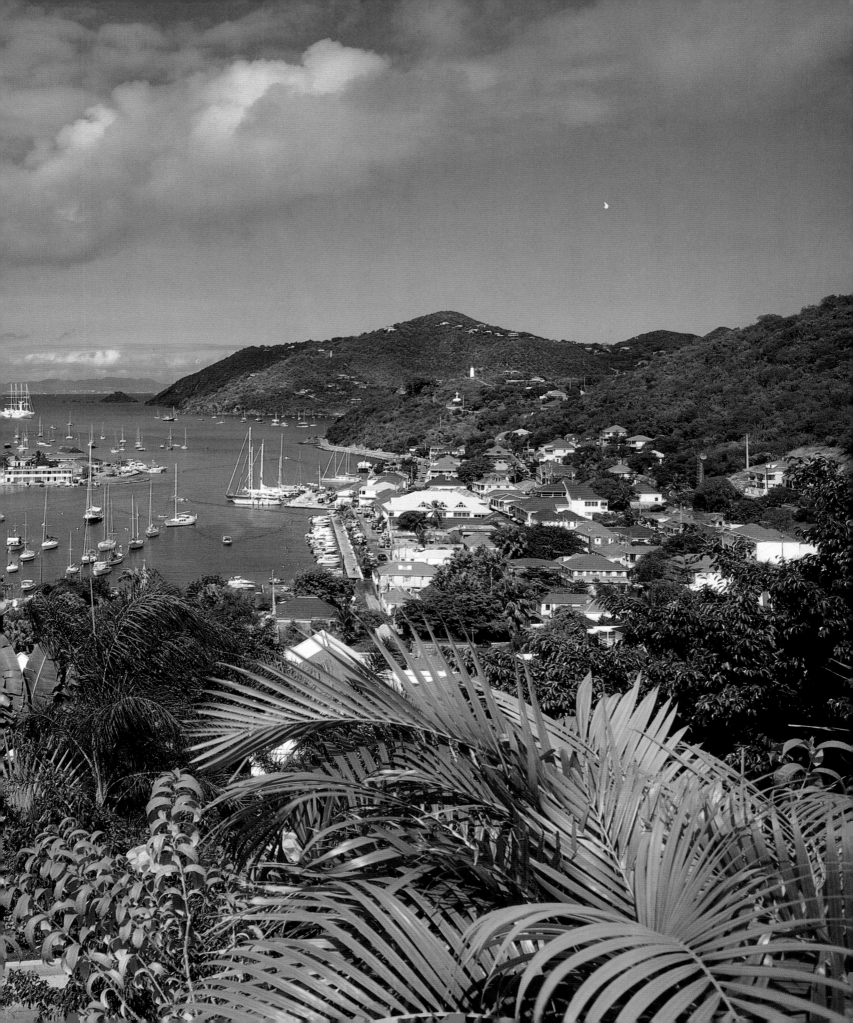

*Text by*
Eugenio Bersani
Lucia Giglio

*Graphic design*
Anna Galliani

*Map*
Giancarlo Gellona

# Contents

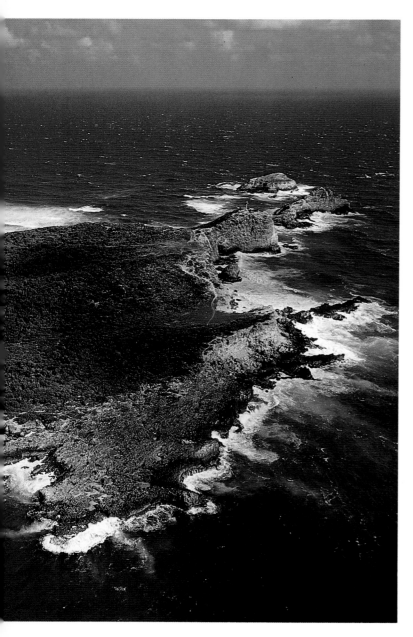

1 *Man of War Bay is one of the loveliest places along the shores of Tobago, the small island which, with Trinidad, forms an independent nation, separated from South America by as little as 6 miles.*

2-3 *Off the southern coast of Cuba is Cayo Largo (in Spanish its name sounds like "long street"), a 90-km strip of unbelievably white coral sand.*

4-5 *St.John, one of the U.S. Virgin Islands, has been described as "an unspoilt tropical paradise": its reputation is borne out by its sparse population (only 3,000), a National Park (since 1956) occupying practically the entire island and assorted coves, inlets and beaches where nature can still be seen in the raw.*

6-7 *The intense, warm colours of the Tropics illuminate the splendid bay of Gustavia, capital of Saint-Barthélemy, a small French Caribbean island. Gustavia is gaining popularity as a tourist destination, but it is a retreat for the rich and famous (the Rockefellers and Rothchilds own large tracts of land here) rather than a playground for the masses.*

8 *On the eastern tip of Guadeloupe is the Pointe des Chateaux, a stunning rocky promontory stretching out into the aquamarine waters of the Caribbean.*

9 *A beautiful face, with features seemingly carved from ebony, peers out on a narrow street in Castries, capital of St.Lucia.*

12-13 *With beautiful beaches just feet away from coral reefs, Tobago is a scuba divers' paradise.*

This edition published in 1996 by SMITHMARK Publishers, a division of U.S. Media Holdings Inc., 16 East 32nd Street, New York, NY 10016.

SMITHMARK books are available for bulk purchase for sales promotion and premium use. For details write or call the manager of special sales, SMITHMARK Publishers, 16 East 32nd Street, New York, NY 10016; (212) 532-6600.

First published by Edizioni White Star. Title of the original edition: Caraibi, preziose gemme dell'Atlantico. © World copyright 1993 by Edizioni White Star. Via Candido Sassone 24, 13100 Vercelli, Italy.

ISBN 0-8317-4494-4

Printed in Singapore by Tien Wah Press.

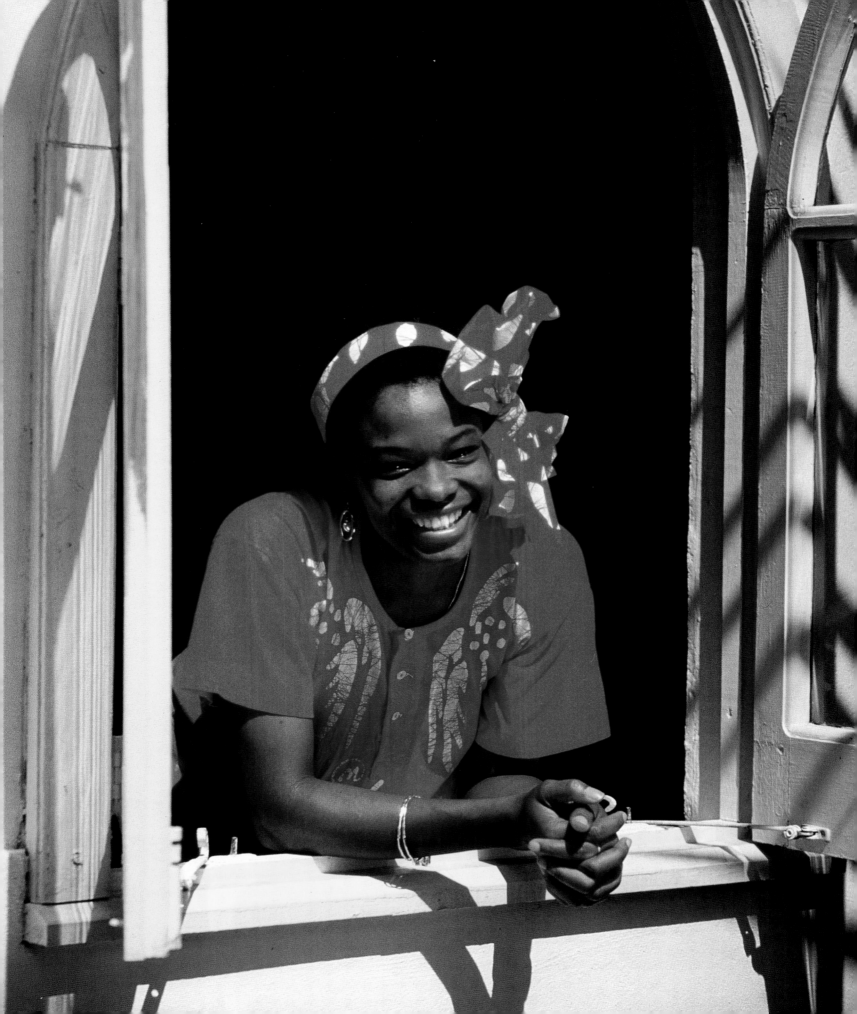

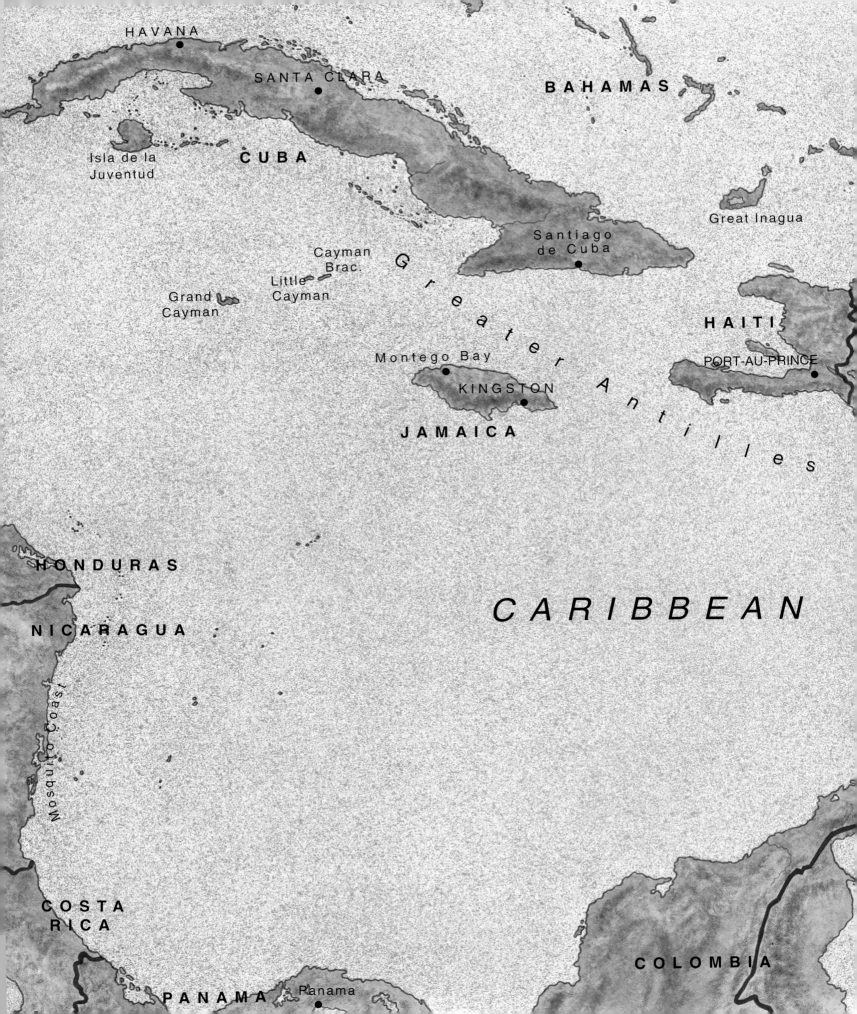

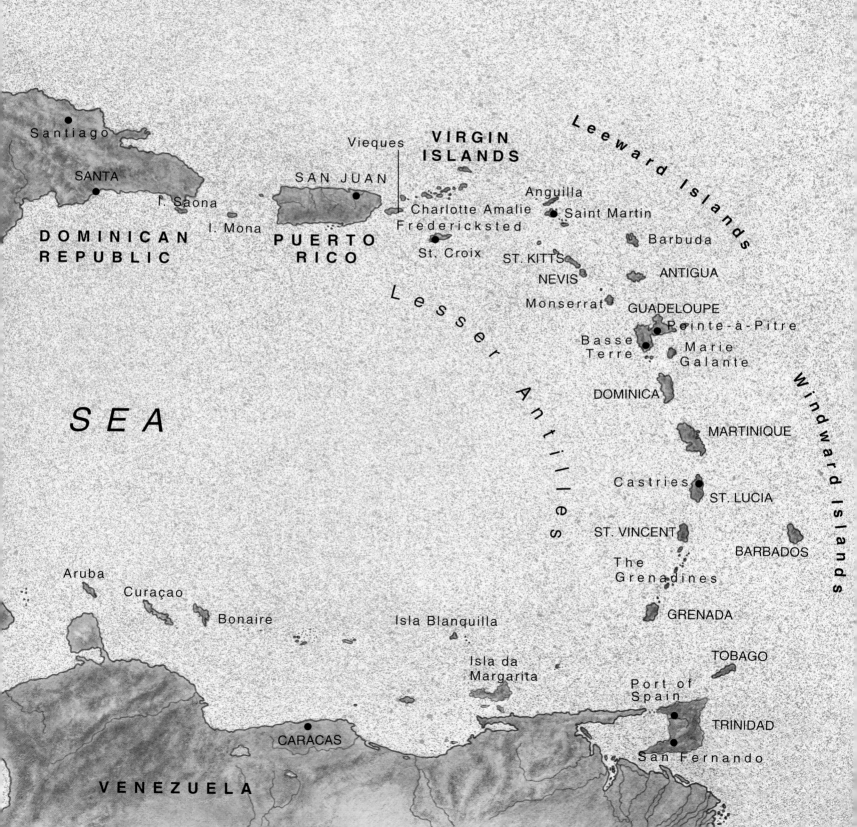

# Introduction

Here in the Tropics, lush vegetation fills every spare inch of space and the burning sun saps every spark of energy. And yet, however fierce the heat, the peoples of the Caribbean abide by their fundamental mission in life: to enjoy themselves. Without an apparent care in the world, they laugh, sing and dance their way through each day. This effervescent approach to life is shared by peoples of widely divergent ethnic origins and cultures, and it is one of their most endearing charms. On any of the islands large and small scattered by some benevolent god between the Tropic of Cancer and the coast of Venezuela, you come across the same brilliant colours, the same smiling faces (however much the physical features of these islands' occupants have varied through the centuries) and, above all, the same irresistible joie de vivre summed up in the pulsating rhythm of intoxicating, sensuous Caribbean music.

This huge archipelago between the north and south of the American continent is comprised of a thousand different worlds. No place on earth offers a greater assortment of exotic landscapes: extinct volcanoes, rain forests, green valleys with plantations of waving sugar-cane, rolling hills, mountain ranges and, of course, the ocean. In the last decade or two it has seemed that this one remaining paradise of modern times is inexorably destined to become a huge secluded haven for tourists in search of sun tans and exotic pleasures. The mythical dimension of these islands, the many legends perpetuated in tales of romance and adventure that have delighted Western readers, appear to be the epilogue of a past now lost for ever. But do the glossy pictures in travel brochures really tell the whole story?

Has the Caribbean's links with its fascinating past been severed for ever? Delving into their history we find that every one of these islands has stirring tales to tell. Their "package tour" image is only surface

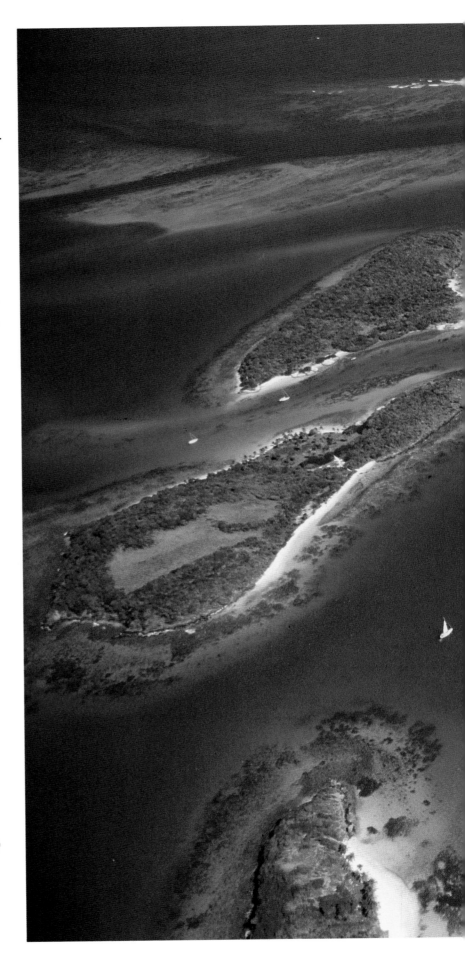

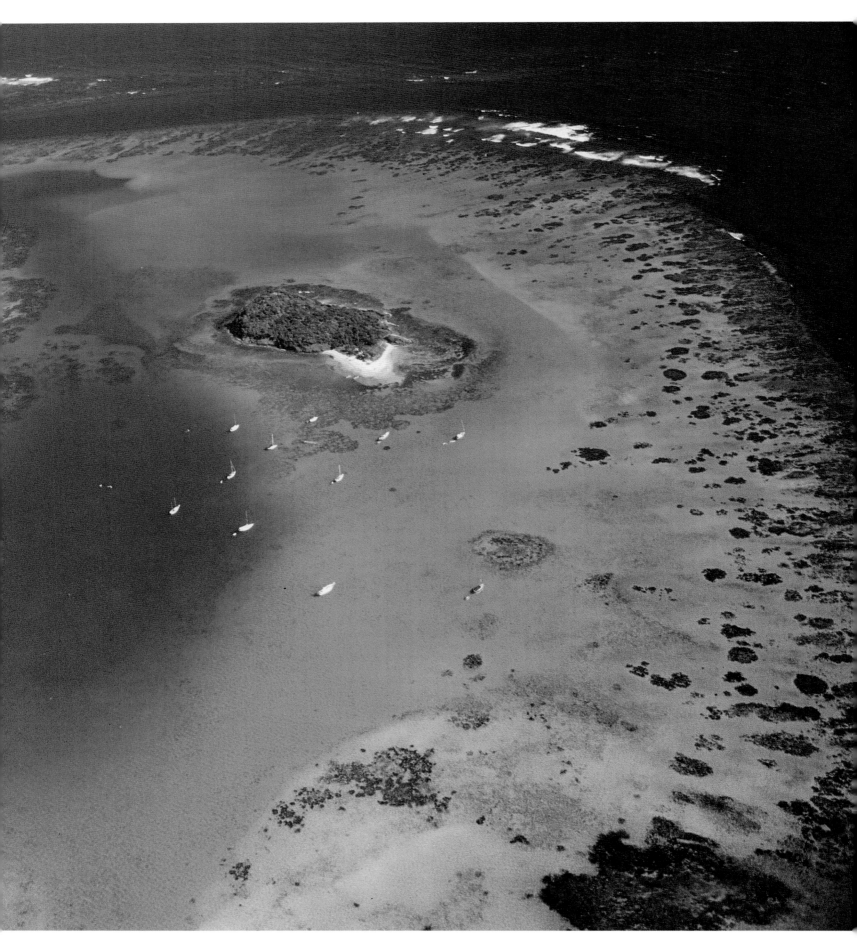

deep. The Antilles are still the legendary lands found by early Renaissance explorers who were searching for the semi-mythical world of Antilia, islands whose existence had been imagined by 15th-century Italian cartographers. Far from being lost, the past of the Caribbean adds a special magic to every aspect of its present. Centuries ago European civilization and black Africa collided and converged here, and the resulting melting-pot is the key to the fascination of the Caribbean today. The Greater Antilles were the scene of fierce battles between Spain, France, England and the Netherlands.

Galleons from the "holy" Christian world of Europe sailed homewards from the harbours of Cuba, Hispaniola (now divided into Haiti and the Dominican Republic), Jamaica and Puerto Rica carrying huge cargoes of gold. For many years Europe's seafaring powers struggled to gain control of these rich, fertile lands. It seemed the Lesser Antilles might escape this same cruel fate since, as they had no gold, the Spaniards considered them of no interest. These islands are small, some of them tiny, but still unspoilt: they include the mysterious Windward and Leeward Islands, magical places where buccaneers and pirates once held sway.

Untamed nature and limited space have held in check the excesses of urbanization and the tourist boom, now all too apparent on the bigger islands; set in the bluest ocean in the world, these places have instead managed to keep intact their original physiognomy, proud and enticingly beautiful. But the disinterest of the great European powers was short-lived.

This time it was the English and French who seized the lovely Windward and Leeward Islands; in the 17th century the first English colony was established at St.Kitts and France took possession of Martinique and Guadeloupe. Even the tiniest islands were found to offer fertile terrain for an effortlessly produced new, green treasure: sugar-cane.

Plantations of the profitable new crop spread throughout the Caribbean region, leading to new conflicts, huge riches for planters and traders and the deportation of many thousands of slaves from Africa. The

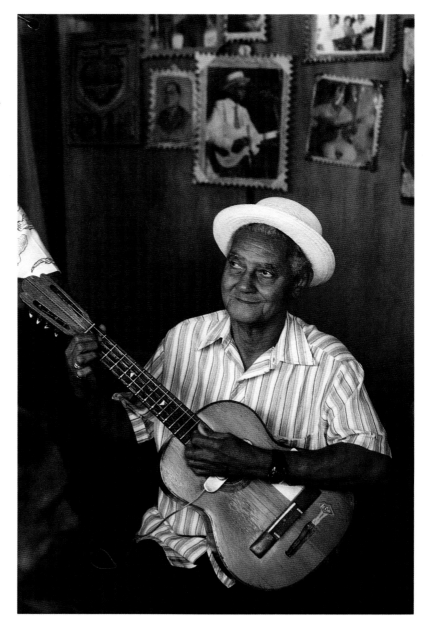

14  *The 'casa de la trova' in Santiago is the most celebrated on the whole island of Cuba: the musicians gathered there every evening offer rousing concerts with their improvised ballads.*

15 top  *No product expresses the spirit of Cuban culture better than cigars and smoking them is more a national passion than a vice.*

15 bottom  *During 'zafra', the sugar-cane harvest, skilled macheteros are joined by thousands of students and office workers who only occasionally handle a machete.*

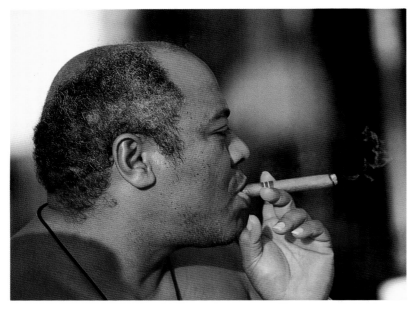

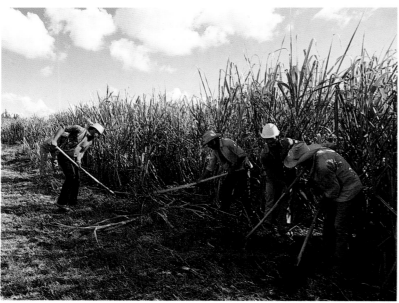

imposition of European culture had a devastating impact on the 'New World'.

Today hardly a trace of the native Amerindians remains; every corner of the islands was turned into a piece of Europe, transplanted in the Tropics, to which the importation of black slaves from Africa added a further ethnic component. The world of the sugar plantations survived only at the cost of bitter and bloody confrontation: on one side, the powerful families of estate-owners who received land and slaves from the authorities; on the other, masses of exploited, ill-treated Africans. This world collapsed towards the mid-19th century, when its foundations were undermined by the combined forces of abolition of slavery and competition from sugar-beet on international markets. A whole way of life disappeared with it. In Cuba, in the midst of the lush greenness of the San Luis Valley, stands the Iznaga Tower: this tall bell-tower is all that remains of the fifty 'ingenios de azucar', the sugar factories which brought prosperity to the city of Trinidad.

It is now a symbol of a long-banished past: from the top of the tower powerful planters kept watch on the slaves toiling among the canes below. The fusion of the disparate cultures of the freed slaves and the descendants of the colonialist settlers resulted in a new cultural manifestation, a unique mélange of traditions and influences which differs from island to island.There is much more to this so-called Creole culture than tropical surroundings and exotica. While it is strongly influenced by the French charm of Martinique, it is also tinged by the pale colours of houses in the Netherlands Antilles and by the neatness and elegance that characterize the British colonies.

Their scenery may be substantially similar but the countries of the Caribbean have wide divergencies in culture, language, ethnicity and creativeness. The thirty million inhabitants of the Caribbean islands are a mix of many races, most prominent amongst them the negroes whose ancestors were brought from Africa as slaves. The spectrum of skin colour is infinite. The palest skins - almost golden - are found in the Netherlands Antilles where there are descendants of Europeans and Chiqueros Indians who, in these parts, survived longer than elsewhere. The pervasive presence of Europe is most noticeable in the capital towns. The beautiful island of Curaçao is Amsterdam in miniature, as sweet as the liqueur distilled here from fragrant oranges.

The old quarters of its main town, Willemstad, are pure delight, with their ornately decorated Dutch-style gabled houses, painted in the palest shades of pink, blue, green and yellow. Since 1634, when these tiny islands were snatched from the Spaniards, Dutch merchants have used the magnificent natural harbour of Curacao to increase their trade. Today it is the largest port in the Caribbean and, in terms of volumes of freight handled, one of the foremost trading ports of the world. The island has a sound economy and widespread prosperity - features not common in this part of the world. In its thoroughly democratic society there is real equality of rights, irrespective of colour and ethnic origin. In Punda, the old trading district of Willemstad, the waterfront still offers an unusual, bustling marketplace - afloat. A line-up of boats which come all the way from Venezuela to sell fish, fruit and vegetables provides shoppers with a somewhat disorderly, but definitely varied row of stalls from which to make their purchases.

But evidence that the Netherlands Antilles are firmly rooted in the modern world is also plentiful. Another snippet of Europe, of a totally different kind, is found in the British possessions: the most northerly of the Leeward Islands were settled peacefully by British colonists as long ago as 1627.

After three centuries under British rule, the populations of these islands - called Bajan - think and live much like inhabitants of Britain: their houses have English-style gardens, they make a ritual of afternoon tea and they are great fans of cricket. Admittedly, the rolling hills and green countryside of Barbados are reminiscent of English valleys and the British-sounding names of the island's villages complete the picture.

A visit to English Harbour, a port of Antigua, makes it easy to understand why the bulldog breed fell for the exotic charms of the Caribbean. This beautiful natural

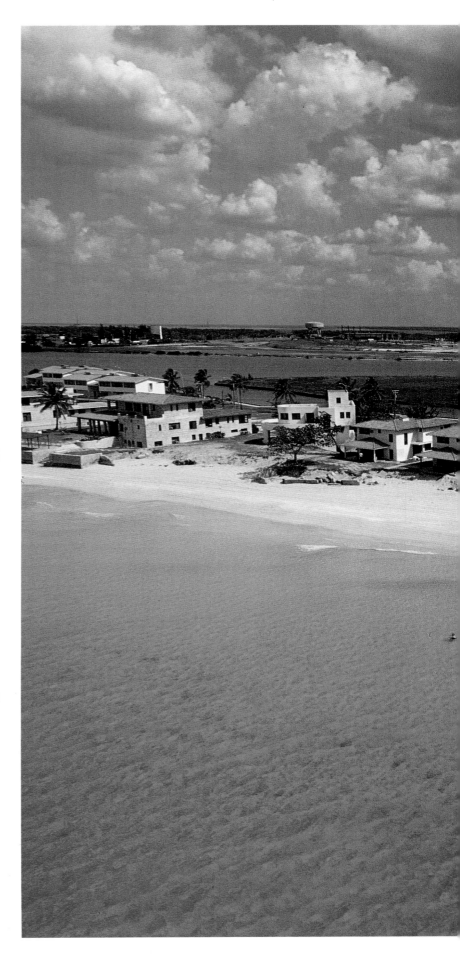

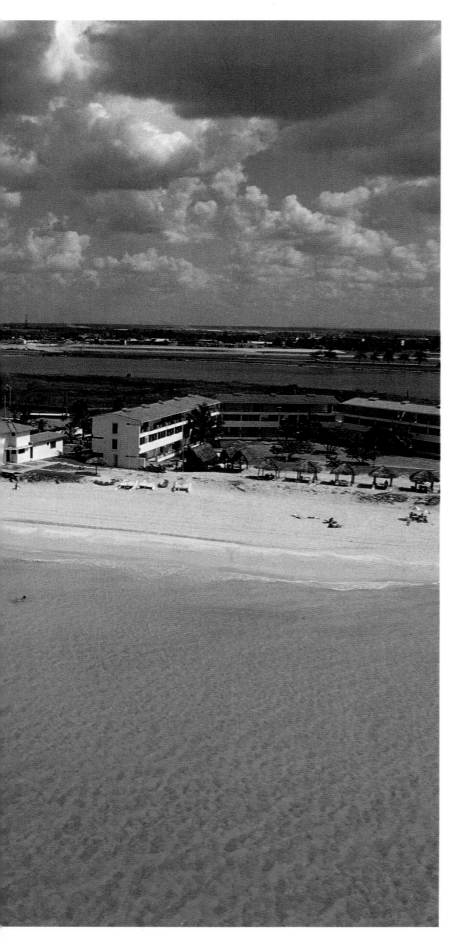

harbour, now a haven for luxury yachts, was once the base of the British fleet in the West Indies: between 1784 and 1787 the officer second-in-command was the future hero of Trafalgar, Admiral Lord Nelson (and the town is practically a shrine to the years he spent here). English Harbour has become a smart, fashionable Caribbean resort, frequented by the rich and famous; its buildings have been restored with British capital, reportedly at the instigation of members of the Royal Family. Old warehouses and waterfront structures have been converted into luxury shops, to ensure that every need of international jetsetters is met in the Caribbean too. Here, as in Curaçao, there is a thriving economy and people live comfortably; unemployment and illiteracy are practically non-existent. Europe's influence is felt again further south, in the French Antilles: Martinique and Guadeloupe - French soil set in tropical waters - almost emanate an illusory fragrance of the Côte d'Azur. But nature here has a wilder, almost cruel side: lording over the islands are still-active volcanoes and the luxuriant vegetation with its dazzling colours - hibiscus, orchids, bougainville - also stems from the fiery veins beneath the craters. Fort-de-France, administrative capital of Martinique, has much in common with many French coastal towns.

It has also acquired some Western vices: upmarket apartment buildings and luxury stores now feature largely. The town itself - birthplace of Joséphine, the splendid Creole who later became Empress of France - is not exceptionally attractive. The splendours of the island are instead seen inland, in a mosaic of tropical forests and plantations, and along its beaches of black sand, under the threatening shadow of its capricious volcano, Montagne Pelée. To the west, scattered in an incomparably blue sea and lulled by the Trade Winds, is another British Crown Colony. The British Virgin Islands are a micro-archipelago of over fifty islands, including atolls, only part of them inhabited and all well worthy of their name. Perhaps in no other part of the Caribbean is nature so splendidly unspoilt: no high-rise hotel developments here, but peace and quiet amid secluded beaches lapped by

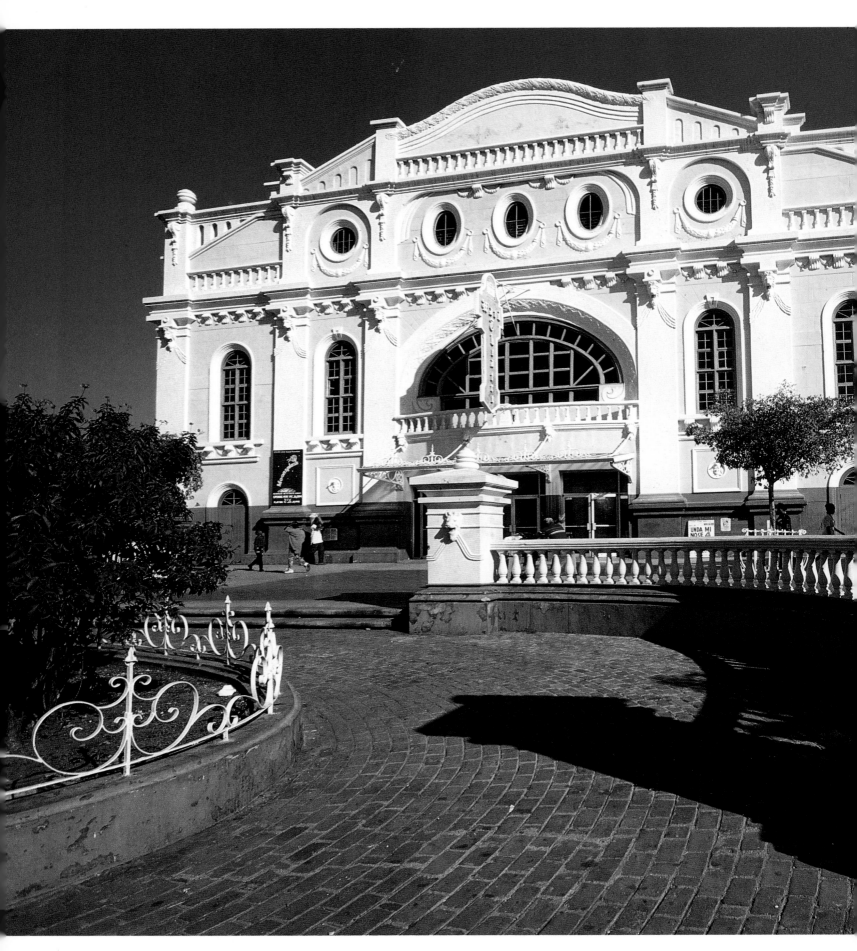

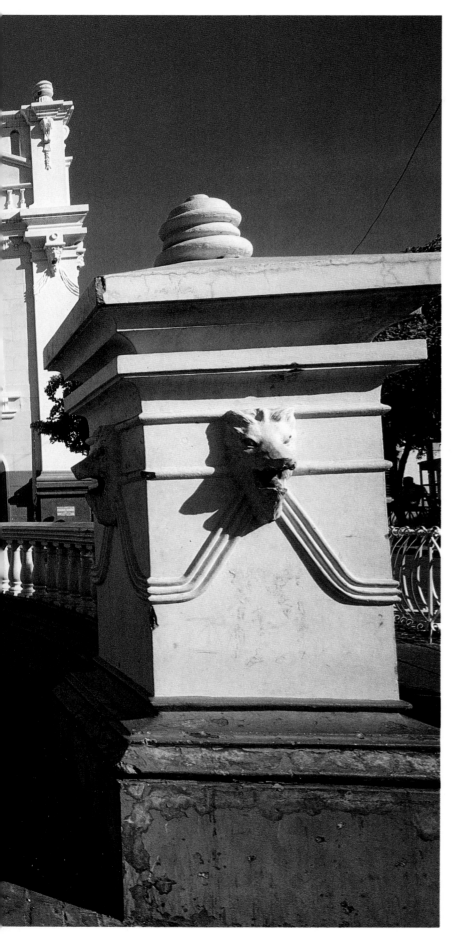

translucent blue water and the stunning lushness of nature in the tropics. Virgin Gorda is the loveliest of the islands, a quiet backwater where there is not really even a proper town: little more than a succession of bays fringed with tall palm trees, against the vibrant green backdrop of a luxuriant Robinson Crusoe forest. The Windward Islands - Dominica, St. Lucia, St. Vincent and Grenada - were also once British possessions, but they all gained their independence in the 1970's.

In these islands - perhaps because of their more southerly position - the mightiness and predominance of nature are tangibly evident at every turn. Amid the picture-postcard settings typical of the Caribbean, Dominica is practically a world apart: its appeal does not lie in white beaches and breathtaking views of conventional tropical splendour. Here the beaches are instead formed of black, volcano-lava sand and the surface of the sea is often more than ruffled.

The harsher side of nature is revealed in places of outstanding beauty, especially inland, where impenetrable forests still cover much of the territory. For adventurous tourists who disdain the beach and its lazier pleasures there is the excitement of exploring the Morne Trois Pitons National Park, in search of animals on the verge of extinction, or bathing in the freshwater springs dotted here and there in the forest. The trails followed by tourists are those first trodden by the Caribs centuries ago and life on the island still proceeds at the leisurely pace of the old-world Caribbean. And as you stroll in the narrow streets of Roseau - the island's largest town, where tourists are still few and far between - the 'dated' atmosphere that the place exudes has an undeniable appeal. Much of the charm of Grenada too comes from its unspoilt natural environment: amid the many extinct volcanoes at the heart of the island are sulphur lakes, rivers and sparkling waterfalls.

Although the island has relatively few beaches, unlike Dominica's they comply with the tropical norm. The loveliest beach is Grande Anse: a two-mile stretch of the finest sand, bordered by unbelievably transparent water. But what sets Grenada apart, with a totally different kind of exotica, is the sweet, heady smell of spices that wafts through the air. The island's home produce - primarily nutmeg, but also saffron, vanilla, ginger, cinnamon and pepper - can be found on sale at the lively Saturday market in St.George's, the capital. It is a very pretty town, once called - in a somewhat unlikely comparison - the Portofino of the Caribbean, maybe on account of the red roofs of the handsome colonial dwellings set against the tropical green vegetation. Or maybe because St.George's lies on the gently sloping sides of an extinct crater, the Carenage, which is a natural harbour and the best anchorage for miles around.

After conflict and violence in the recent past of Grenada, with intervention by US marines in 1983, tourism is now expanding, but unhurriedly and with respect for the island's character: no sprawl of concrete and legislation prohibiting buildings that stand higher than the palm trees.

Sailing westwards we come to the Greater Antilles, larger islands whose past riches were the cause of the bloodiest battles. Here, starting from white settlers and black slaves, Europe and Africa have mixed and mingled over the centuries to create a multi-racial society, an exceptionally rich amalgam of different lands and influences. The contrasts and fusions are most striking in the largest islands. Colonial cities, palaces once occupied by Spanish nobility, baroque cathedrals, entire quarters of Havana, Trinidad and San Juan co-habit with culture and religion of African origin. The splendour of the colonialist era is now gone and its remains are tinged with melancholy and decay. It is sad to stroll down narrow streets of Havana Vieja at dusk and to sense the presence of silent gardens, overwhelmed by tropical vegetation, behind the crumbling façades. Our imagination is stirred and we can picture passionate love scenes of the past, destined to come to a tragic end. But our mental wanderings are interrupted by the sound of music, emerging from the most unexpected corners. Its cheerful notes banish our pensive mood. The very essence of black Africa explodes in music which has even the feet of awkward Westerners moving to its beat. This irresistible music is perhaps the culminating manifestation of the

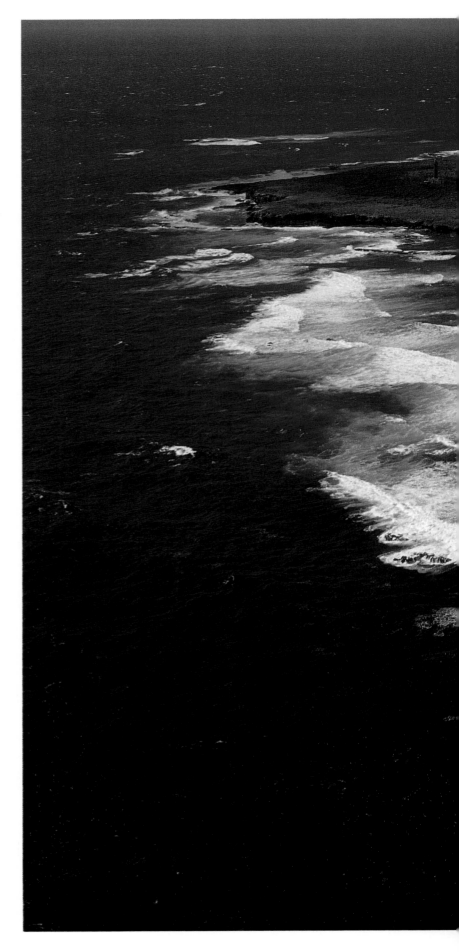

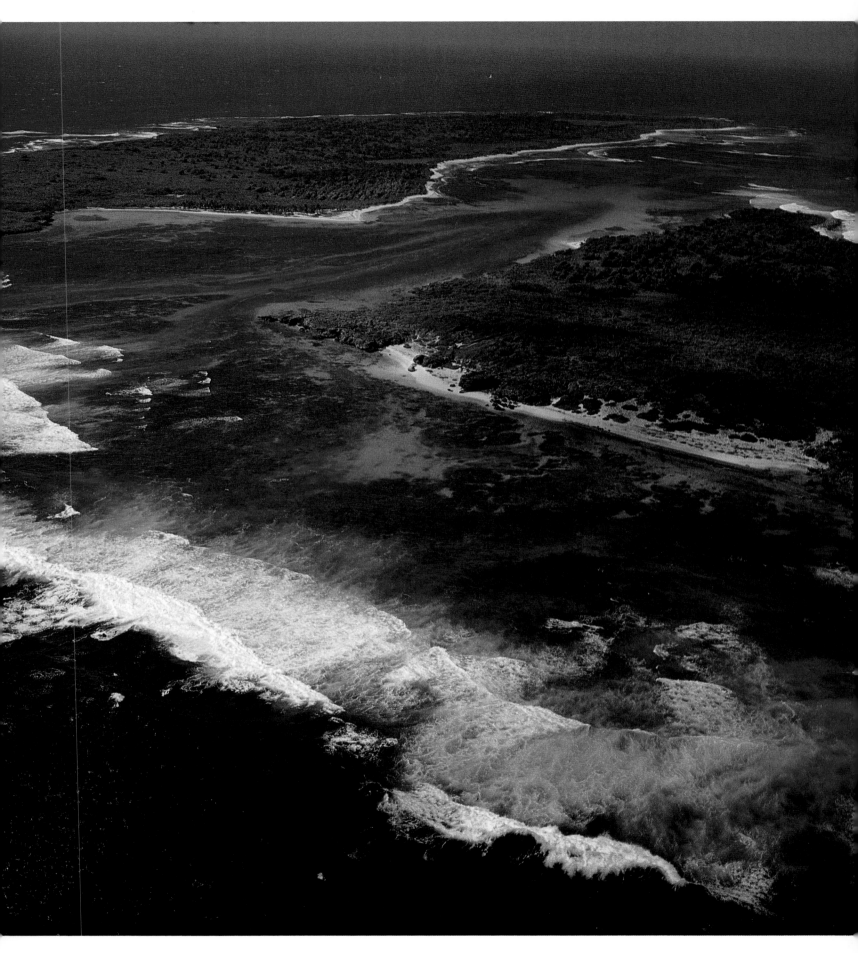

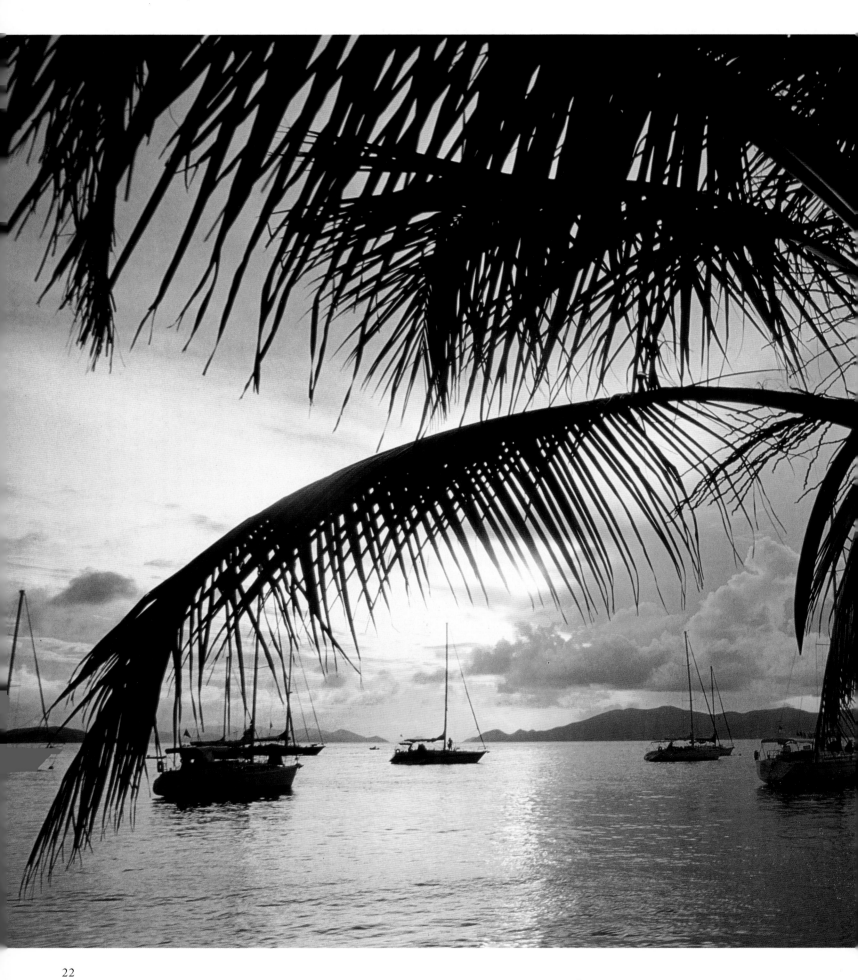

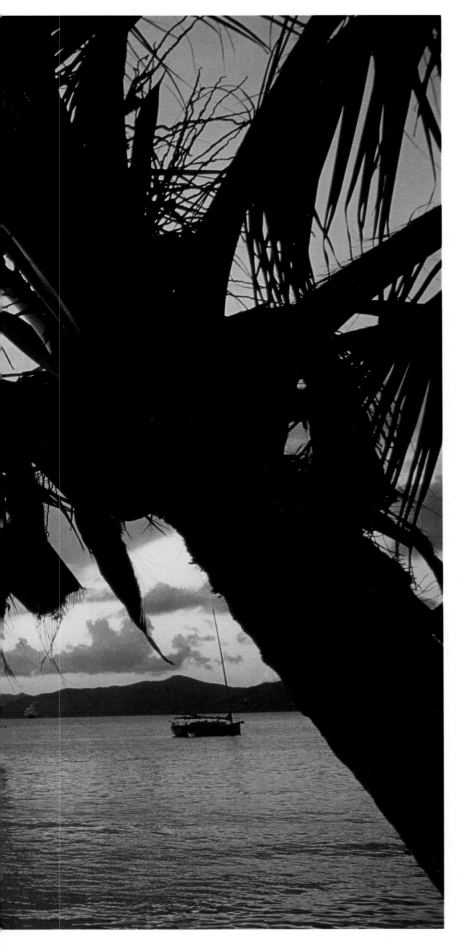

amalgam between whites and blacks, between Europe, Africa and the Caribbean. The cultural influence of the black population is most evident in the poorer districts of Havana or in cities and towns further south - Santiago, Trinidad, Baracoa - where burning sun and hot-blooded people can be an explosive combination. Here music and ritual are indivisible: from their African homeland the black slaves brought tribal music and religious cults which, in the New World, met with the Roman Catholicism of the Conquistadores. The outcome was a strange and complex religious and cultural syncretism in which 'oricha', (African divinities) are identified with Catholic saints. Against the rhythmic beating of drums, the gods of the Bantu and Yoruba tribes have been attributed the external appearance of Christian saints.

In the Roman Catholic churches of Havana - San Gesu de Miramar and Virgin de la Mercede - worshippers absorbed in prayer wear the colours, beads and emblems of the oricha. They are followers of the Santeria cult who worship one of the many African divinities; according to their beliefs, Christian baptism is required before baptism by the 'santero', the priest of the African cult. It is a strange and fascinating world. At Regla, in the eastern suburbs of Havana, is the church of the Virgin de Regla, a black madonna also identified as an oricha: Yemaya, the black goddess of water. Don Angel Perez Vareta, the church's Roman Catholic priest, tolerates this situation and accepts it as normal that the Madonna and Yemaya exist as a single entity in the minds of his flock. Africa is also alive in Guanabacoa, a run-down part of La Habana del Este, where the "high priest" of the Afro-Cuban cult lives.

The home of Enriquito, a powerful 'babalao', is a shrine to Saint Lazarus: this Catholic saint, a cripple, is also 'el santo milagroso' or Babalu Aye, a potent oricha to whom believers turn when close to despair.

As we explore the islands of the Caribbean - discovering their history, magic and mystery - the stereotyped image of the holiday makers' playground fades. Much more than an idyllic combination of sun, sea and sand, these islands embody the very essence of nature, its harsh realities as well as its warmth, as is surely fitting for a garden of Eden. And it is in this that their true charm and beauty lie.

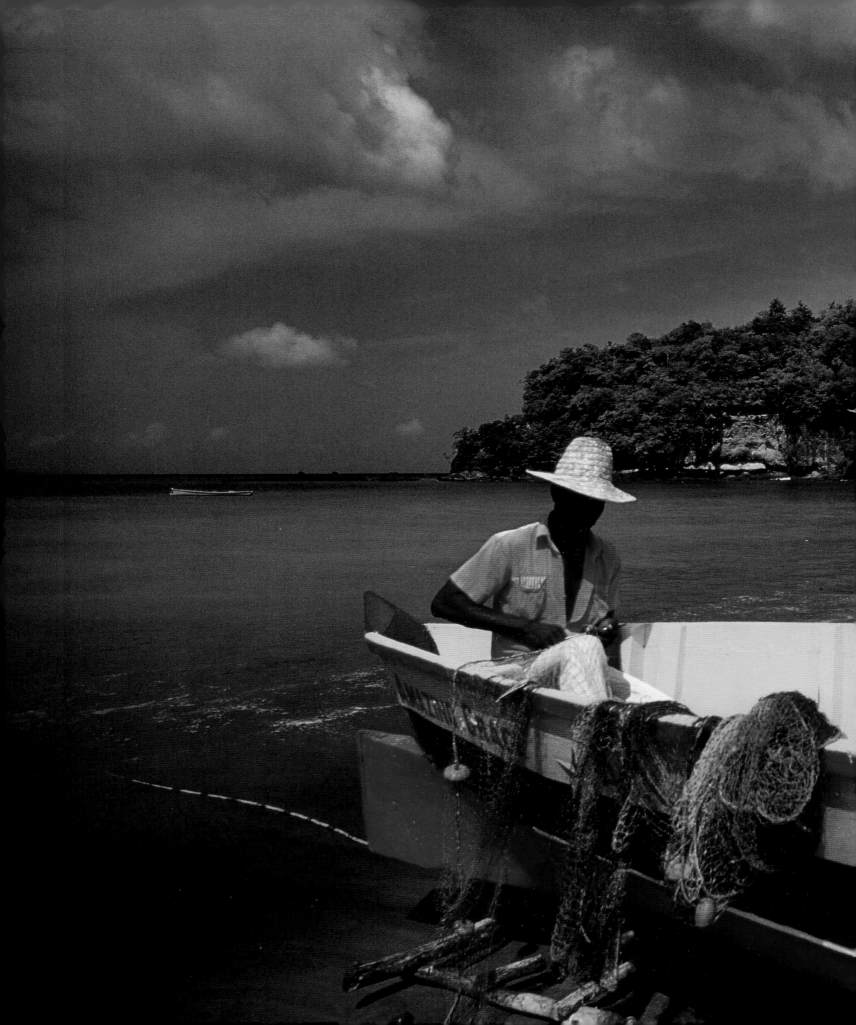

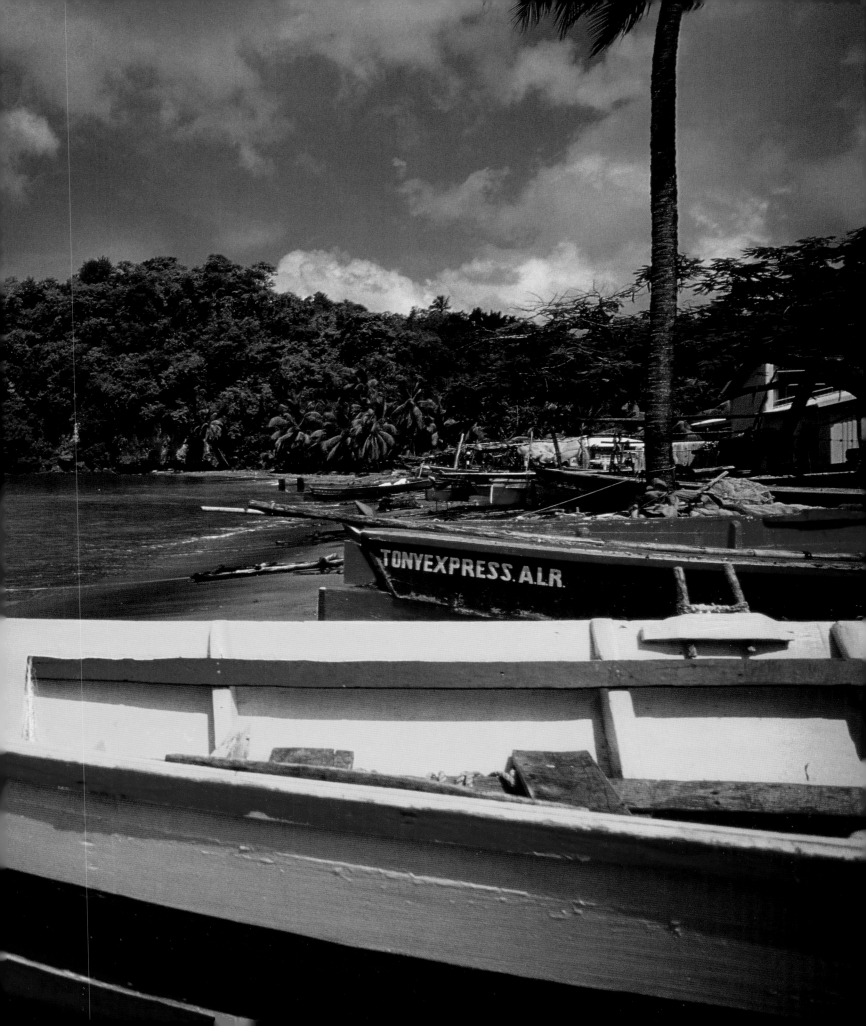

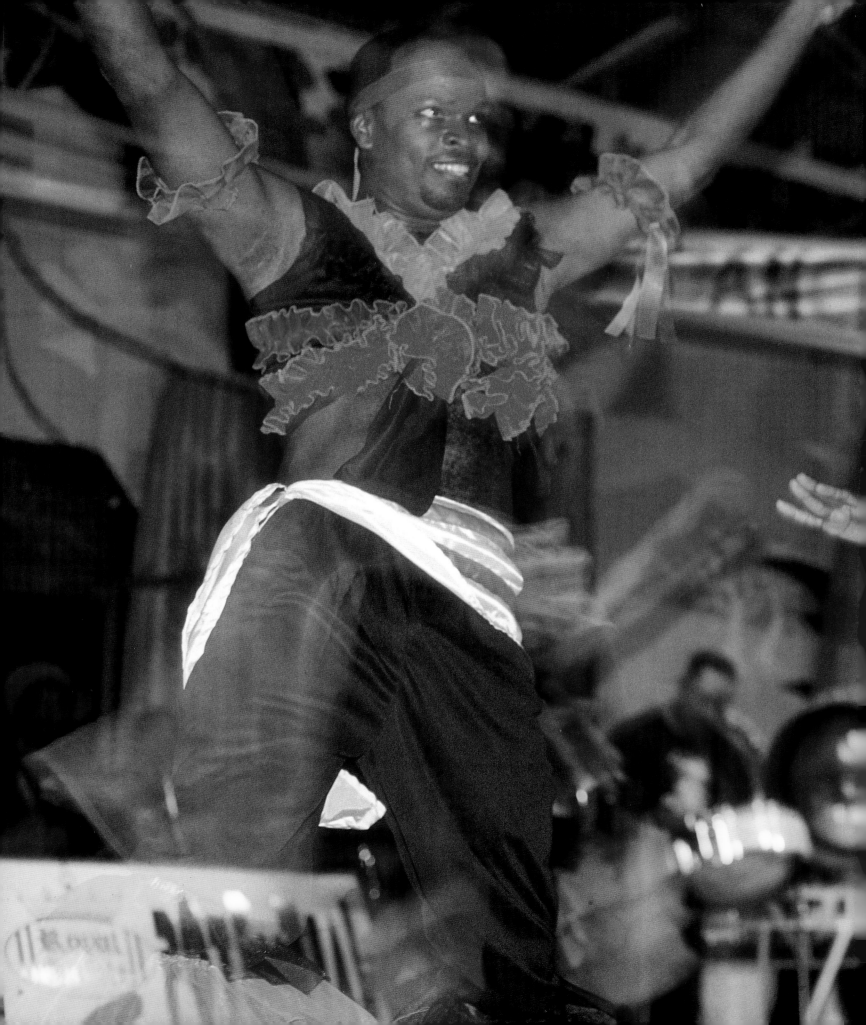

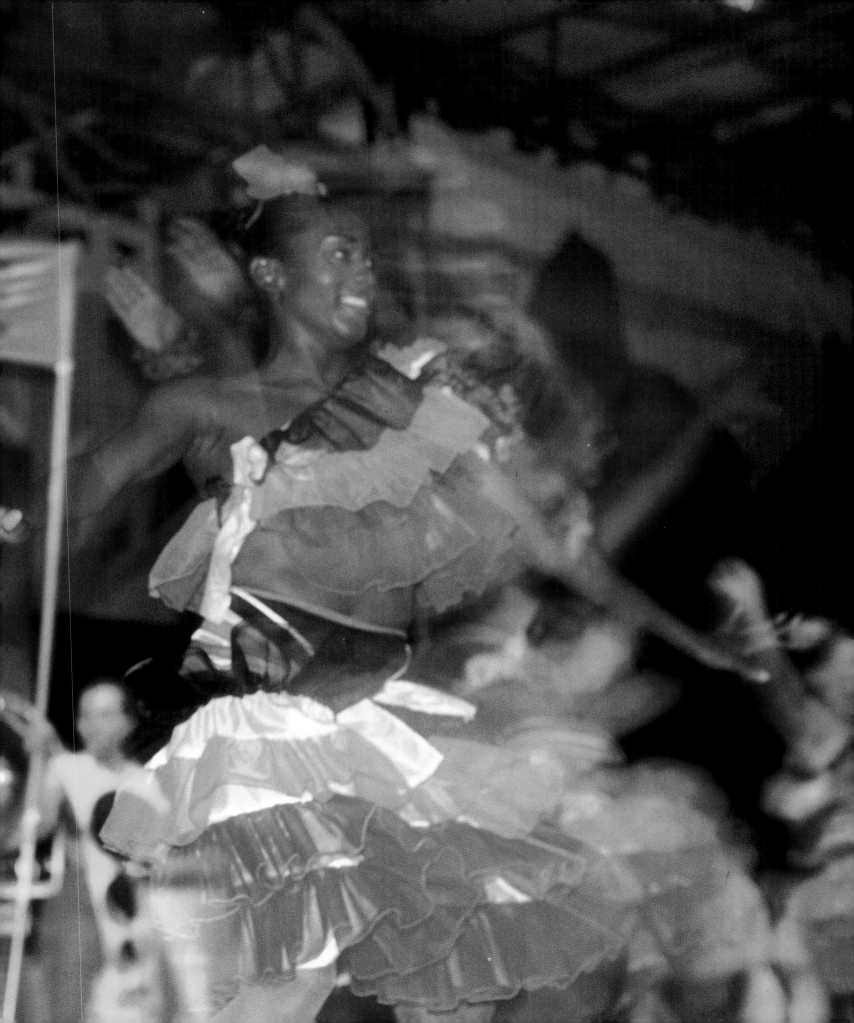

# A Taste of the Colonies

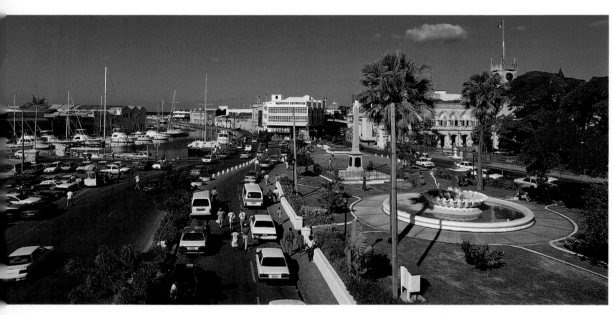

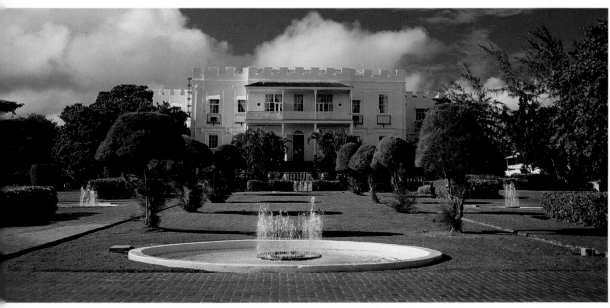

28 top  *The modern harbour and Western-style public gardens are evidence of the British origins of Bridgetown, capital of Barbados.*

28 bottom  *Sam Lord's Castle, in Barbados, was built in 1818 as a prestigious residence for a rich pirate, Samuel Hall Lord.*

29  *Beyond an elegant wrought-iron gate stands the imposing presidential palace of Santo Domingo.*

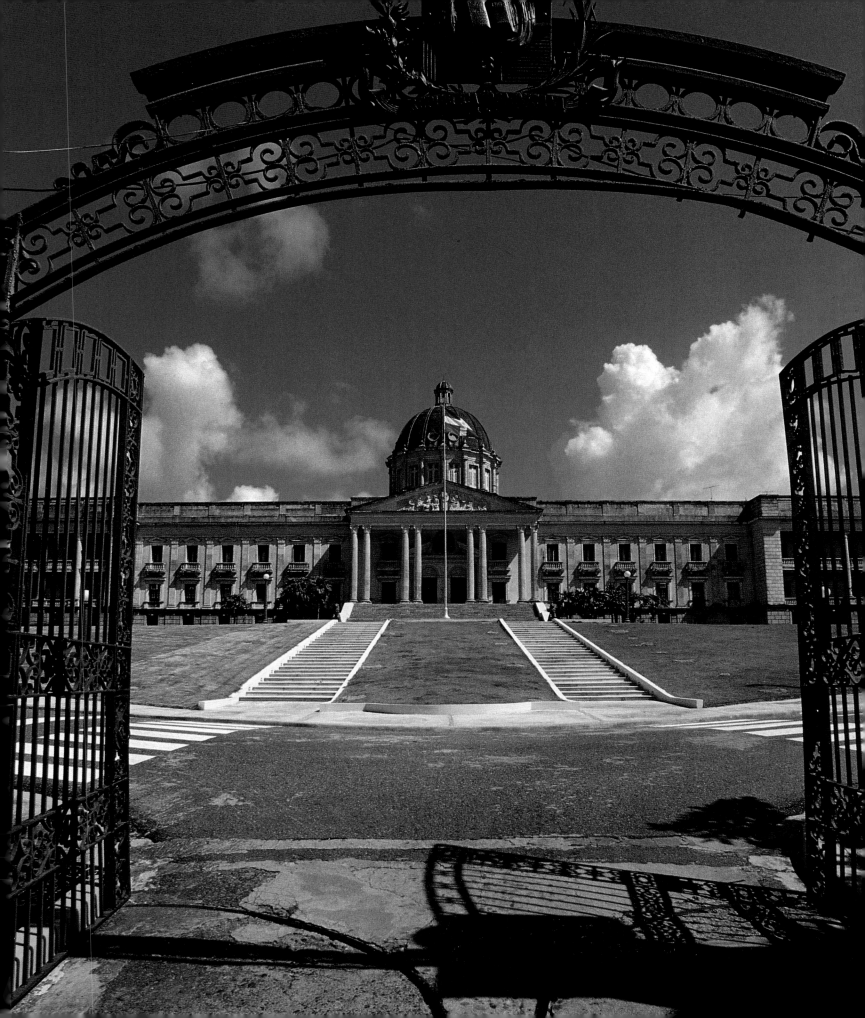

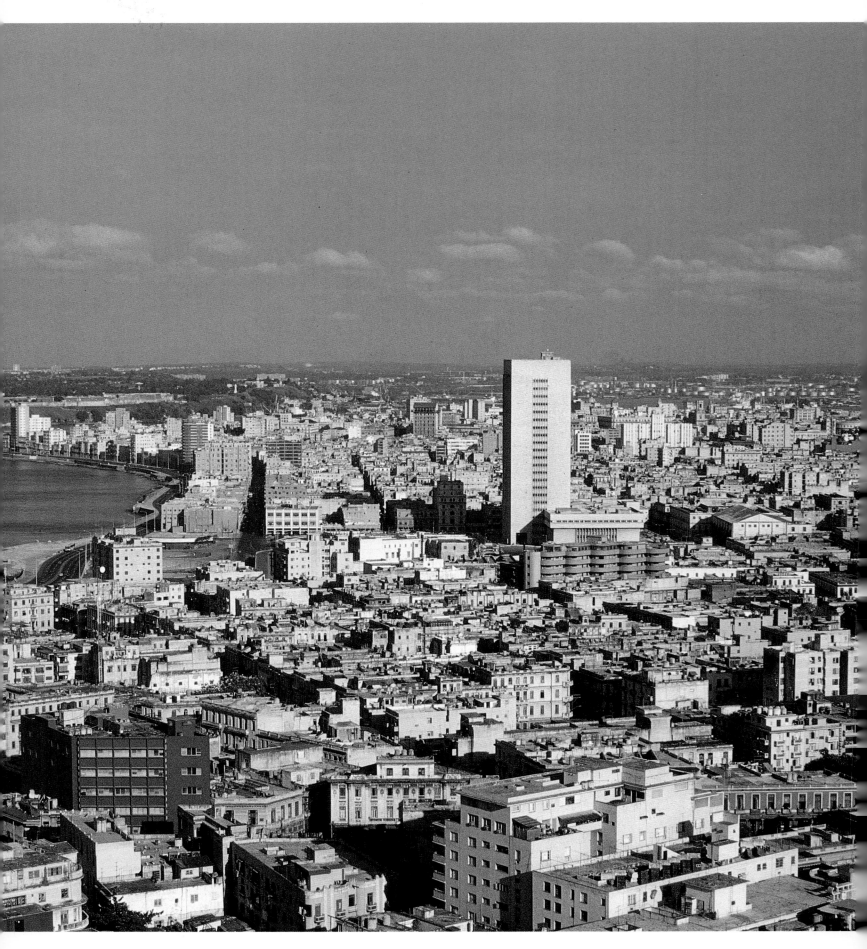

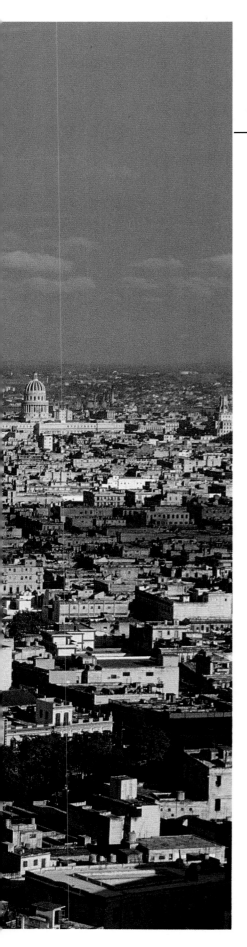

# The fascination of Havana

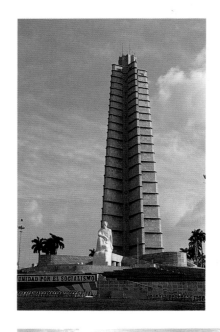

30-31 *Stretching slothfully oceanwards is the urban sprawl of Havana: with a population of over two million it is one of the largest cities of Central America.*

31 top *Dominating one side of the immense Plaza de la Revolucion is the monument to José Martí, Cuban poet and national hero.*

31 centre *When rich US citizens fled the island after Fidel Castro's 1959 revolution, they left many cars behind; the one shown here is a splendid (and lovingly cared for) Cadillac sports model.*

31 bottom *In one of the most modern districts of Havana is the 'City of Sport'; physical education and strong sporting traditions have an important place in the life of Cuban people.*

32-33 *The Castillo de San Salvador de la Punta is one of the monumental fortresses built by the Spanish at the end of the 16th century to defend Havana and its bay.*

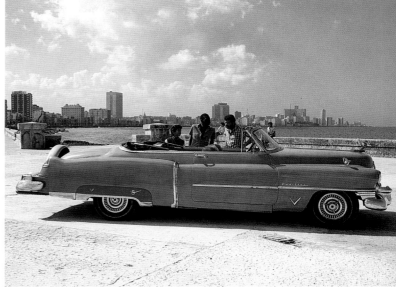

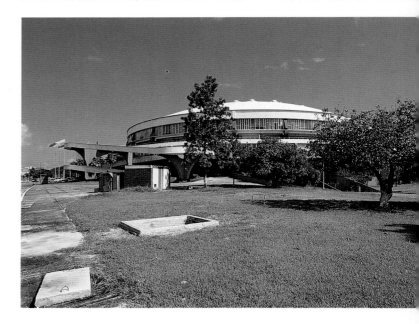

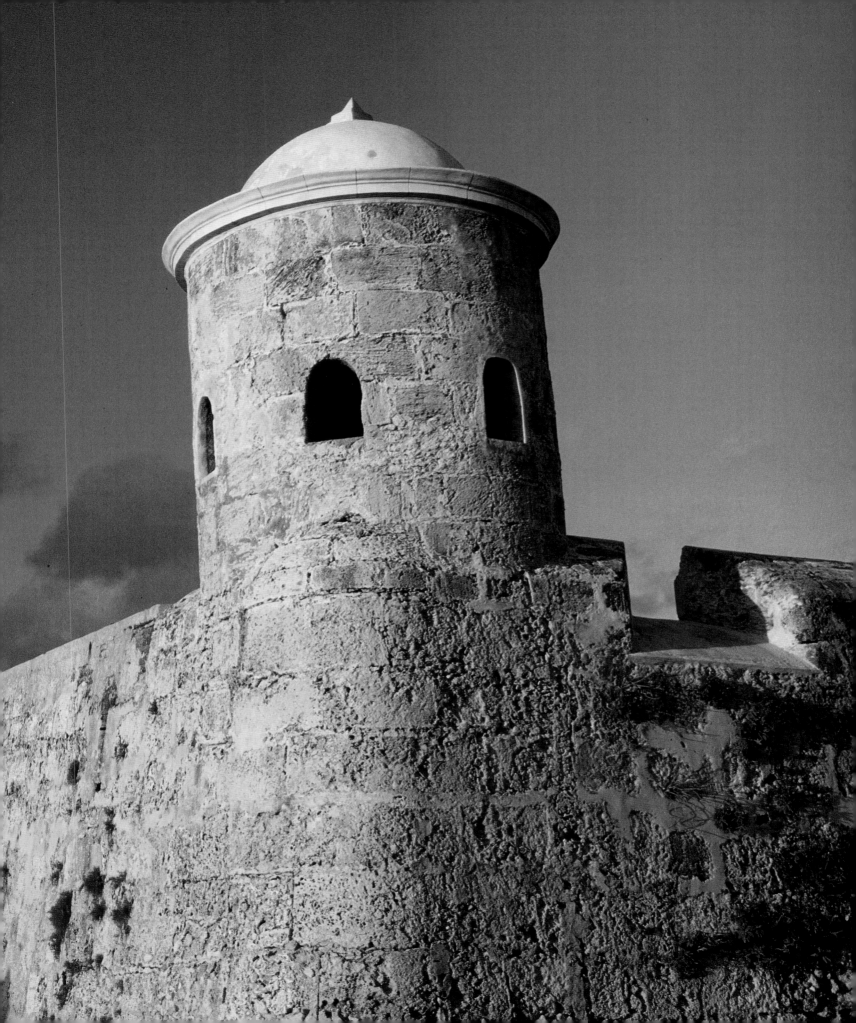

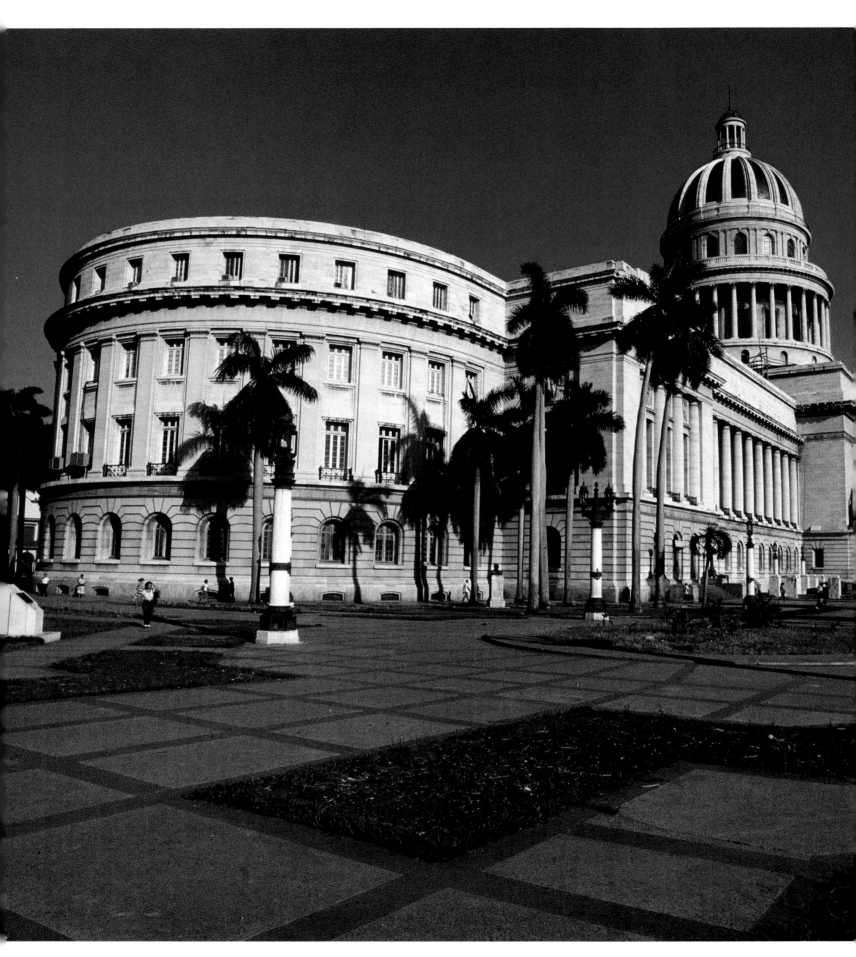

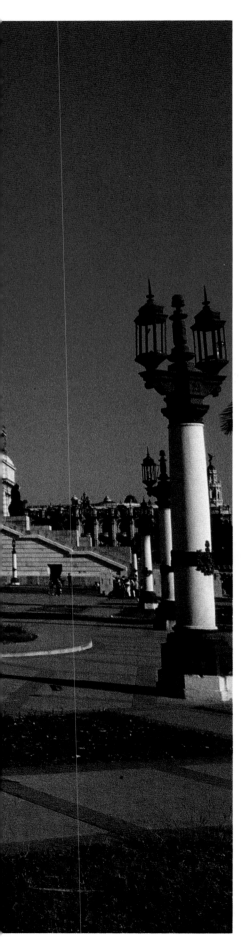

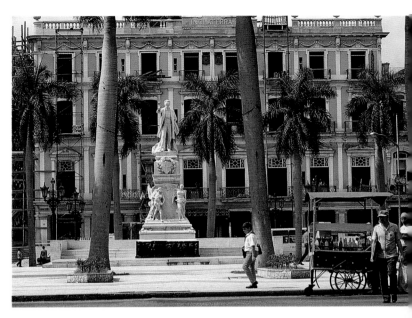

34-35 *With its neoclassical architecture, the imposing Capitolio Nacional, built in 1929, is clearly a copy of Washington's Capitol.*

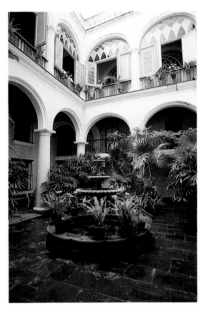

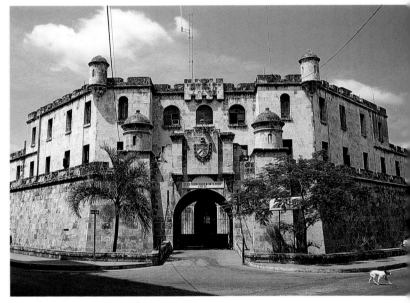

35 left *Fountains, palm trees and discreet ornamentation add to the charm of hundreds of shady inner courtyards in the colonial buildings of Havana Vieja.*

35 top right *The lovely square of the Parque Central is of 19th century origin. Pictured here behind the statue of José Martí, at the centre of the rectangular square, is the delightful façade of the Hotel Inglaterra.*

35 centre right *Presiding over Havana Vieja is an imposing military edifice, a reminder of the many wars and struggles that have coloured the island's past.*

35 bottom right *Spanish taste and American colonial style have together produced the distinctive architecture of Havana's numerous monumental buildings.*

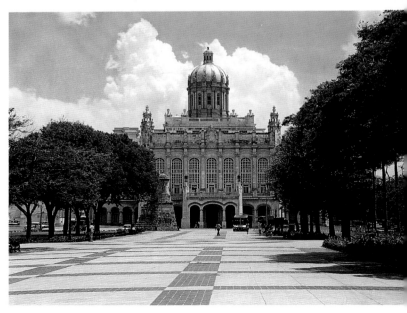

# Trinidad and Santiago, pearls of central and southern Cuba

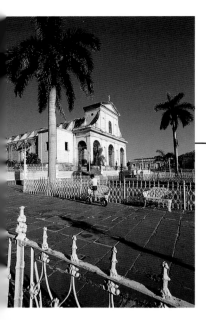

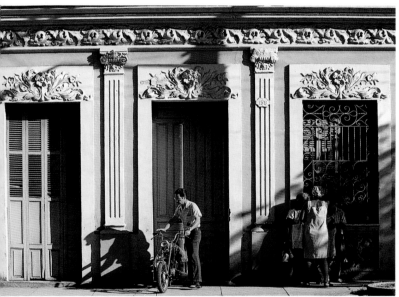

36 top  *One of the cathedrals of Trinidad, a city rich in art and history; its magnificent old centre is one of the best preserved in Latin America.*

36 bottom  *Neoclassical architecture and pastel colours complement each other in the façade of this attractive building in Santiago de Cuba.*

36-37  *The Bahia di Santiago has one of the most sheltered harbours on the island of Cuba; it was from here that Conquistadors Cortez and Pizzarro set sail for South America.*

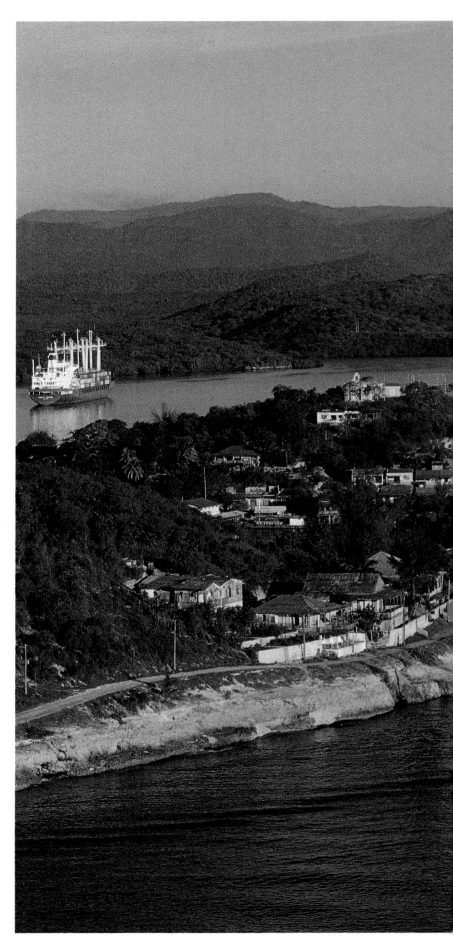

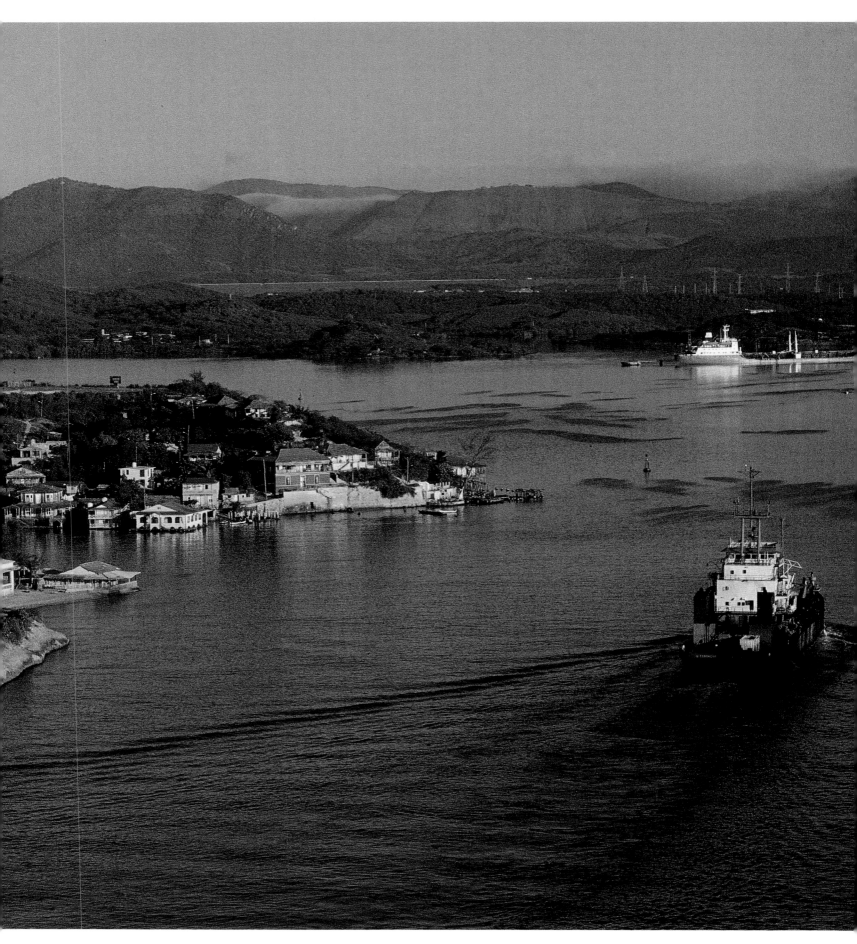

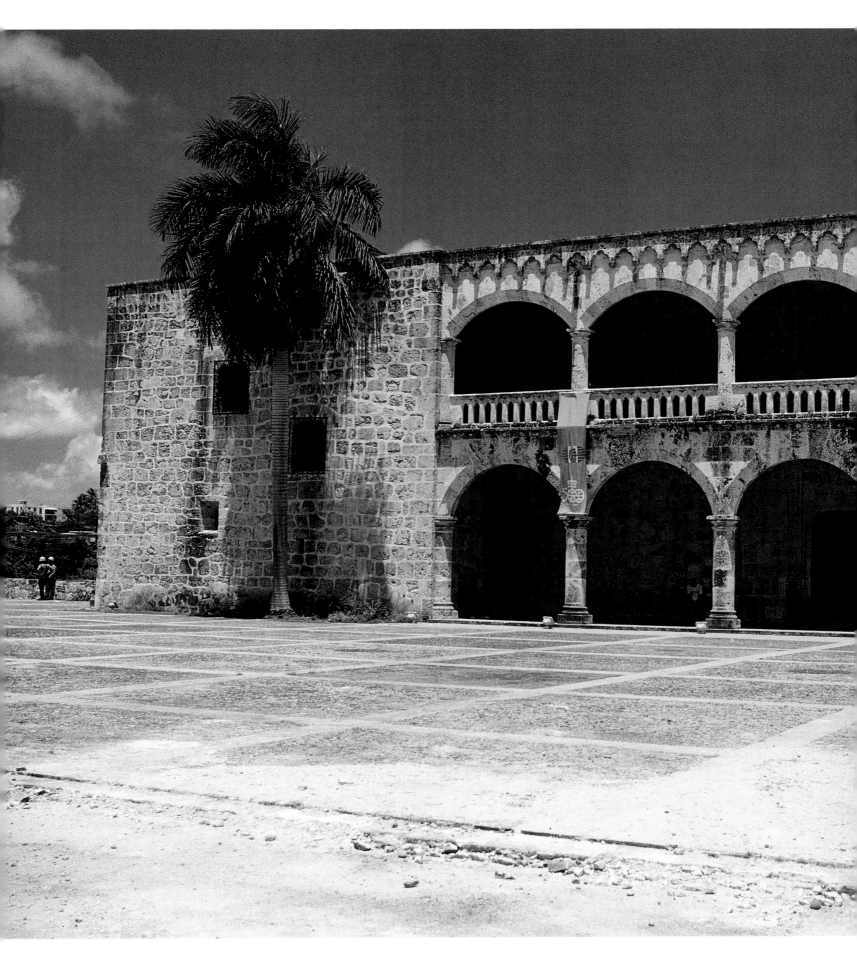

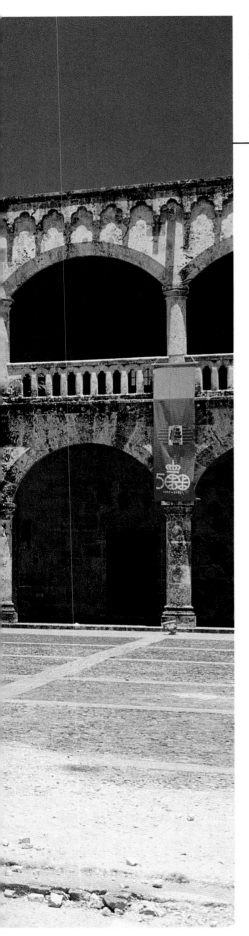

# Santo Domingo, the oldest European settlement

38-39  *Built in 1510 by viceroy Diego Colon, son of Christopher Columbus, the Alcazar de Colon is one of the most interesting remnants of Santo Domingo's former splendour.*

39 top  *Inside the Alcazar is the richly endowed residence of the governor of Hispaniola; after the island's discovery, Santo Domingo continued to be its cultural and political centre for a very long time.*

39 bottom  *The Torre dello Homenaje - 'the tower of tributes' - is part of the fortress sited on the banks of the Rio Ozama.*

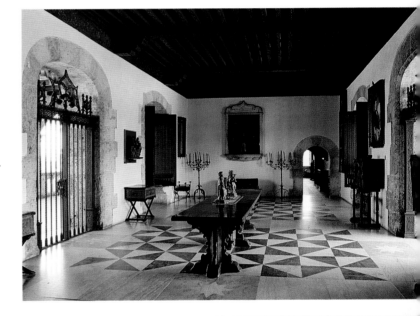

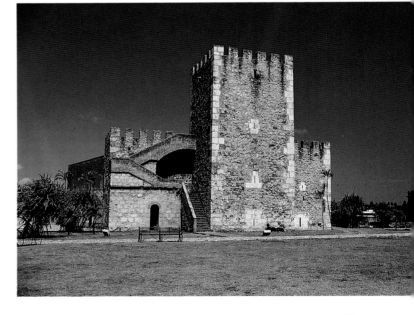

# Enchanting cities of the Caribbean

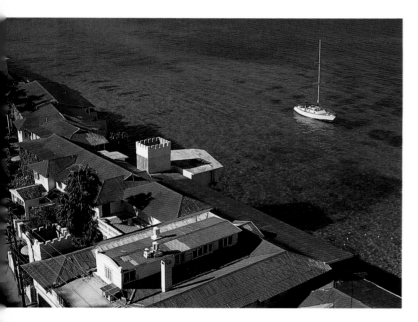

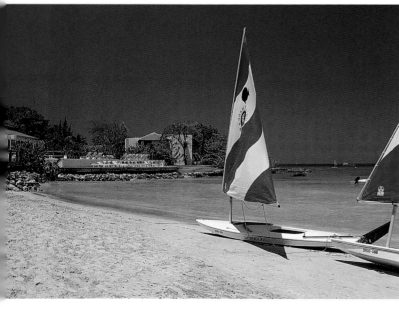

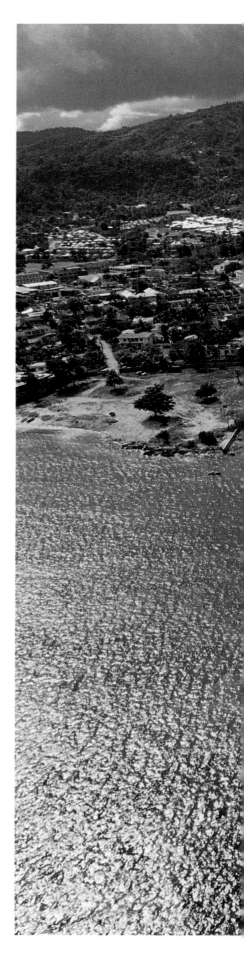

40 top *Montego Bay is Jamaica's second biggest town: a lively and popular international tourist resort, it is also a important centre of trade.*

40 bottom *The luxurious Club Gran Lido is one of the gems of Negril, a fashionable Jamaican resort which boasts almost 7 miles of beach.*

40-41 *As can be seen from this panoramic view, Ocho Rios is a modern resort town, much frequented for its excellent hotels and up-to-the-minute facilities.*

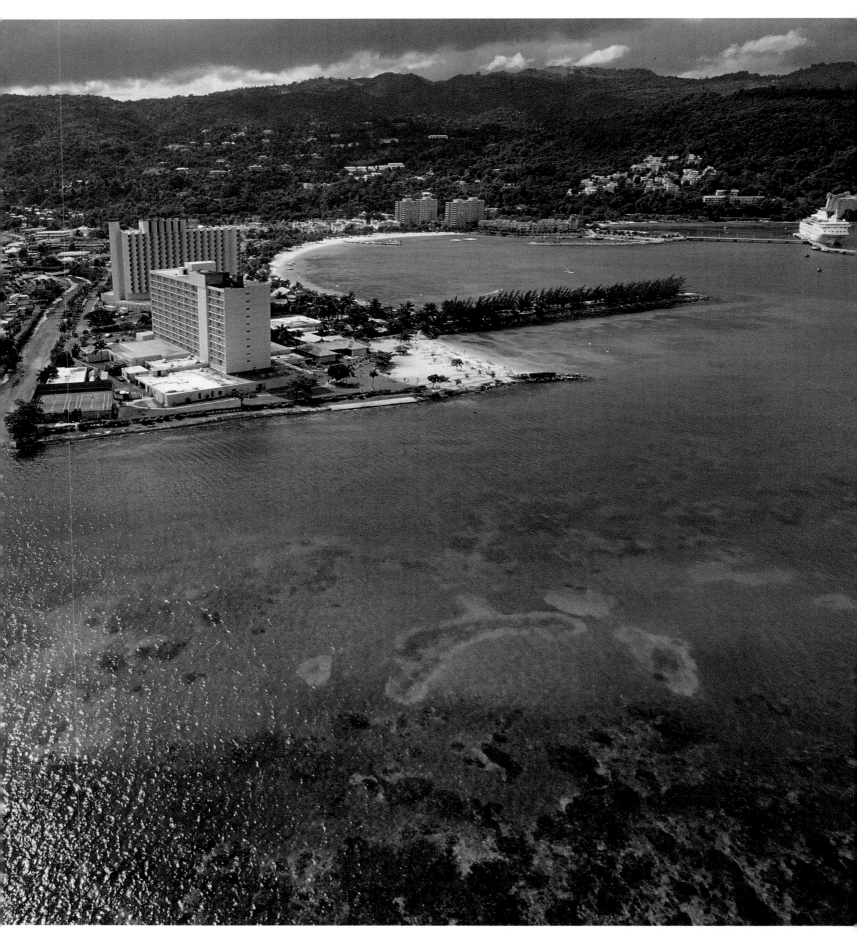

# Traces of war in the heart of the tropics

43 top *The ruins of Fort Fleur d'Epée dominate the coast road close to Pointe des Chateaux, in Guadeloupe.*

42 *At Fort-de-France in Martinique, the French flag flies from the bastions of Fort St.Louis: this magnificent fortress dates back to the 17th century.*

43 bottom *Built in the 1600s, Fort Frederik overlooks the small port of Frederiksted which lies about 16 miles from Christiansted in St. Croix.*

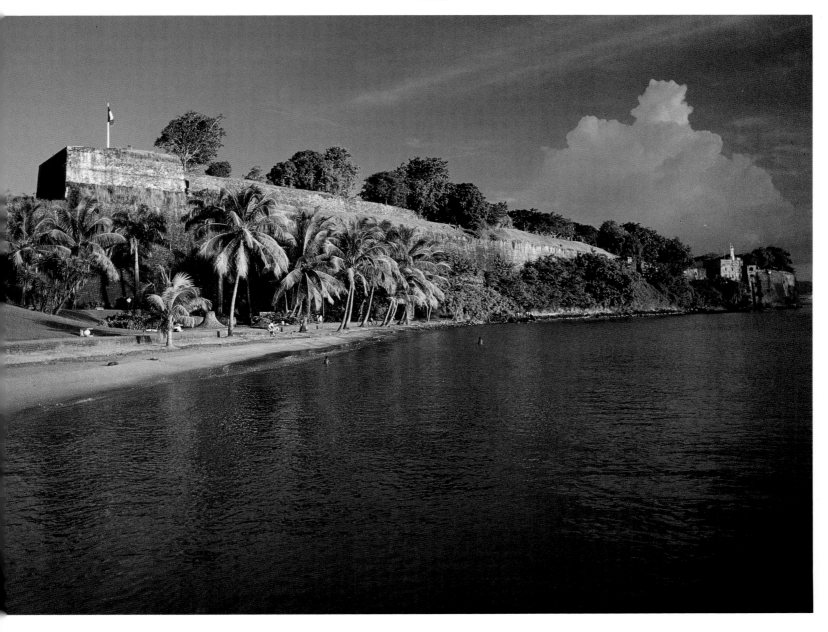

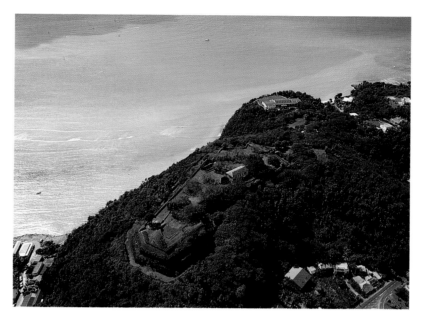

44-45 *The war memorial of Pointe-à-Pitre in Guadeloupe stands in the centre of the town, surrounded by typical colonial buildings with elegant balconies.*

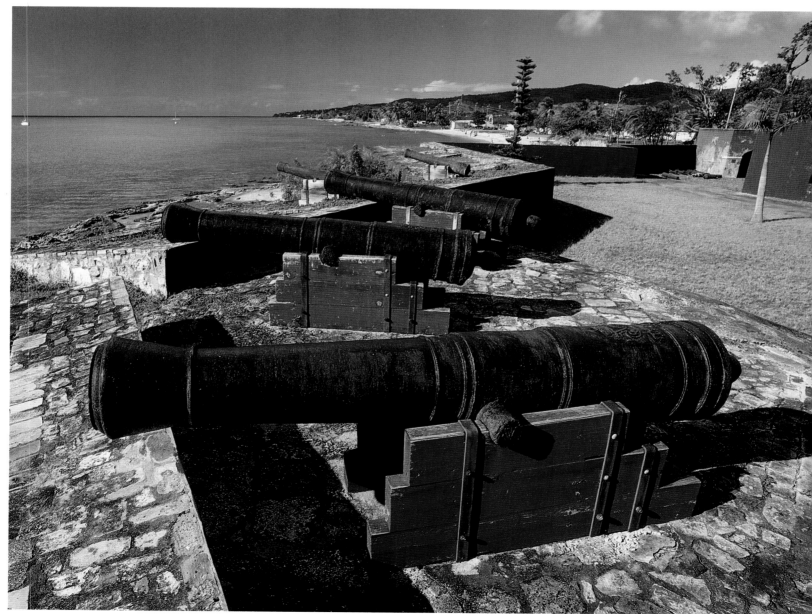

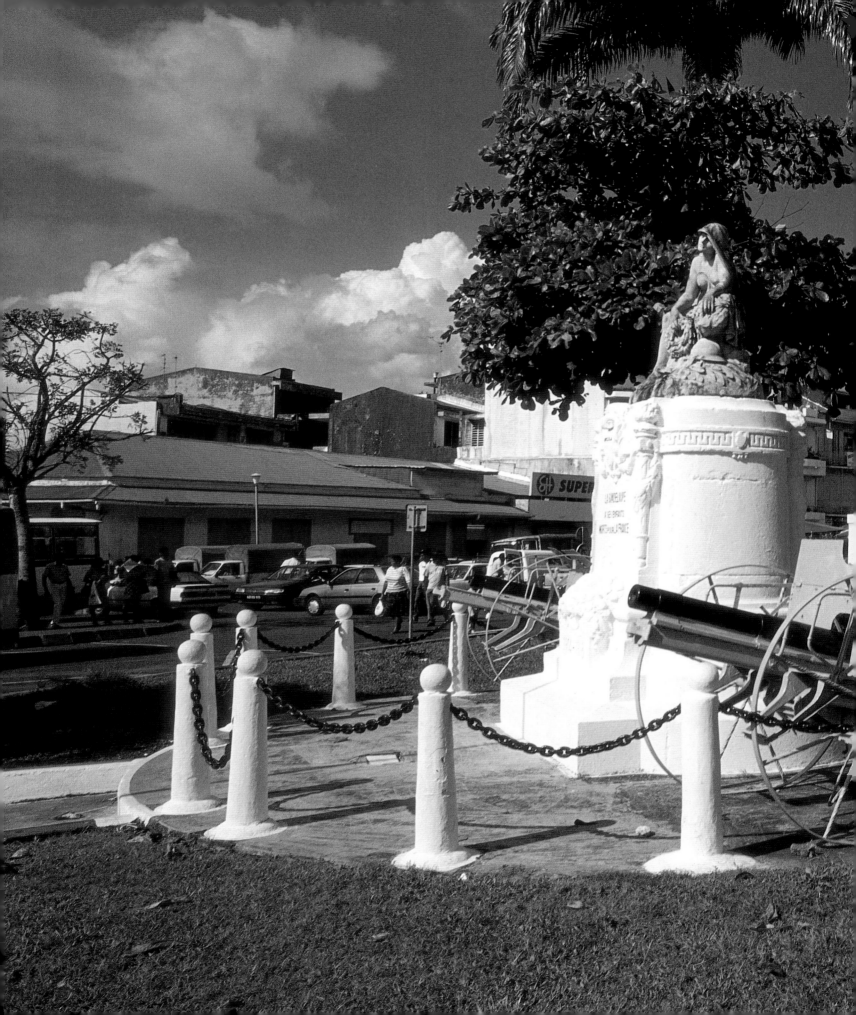

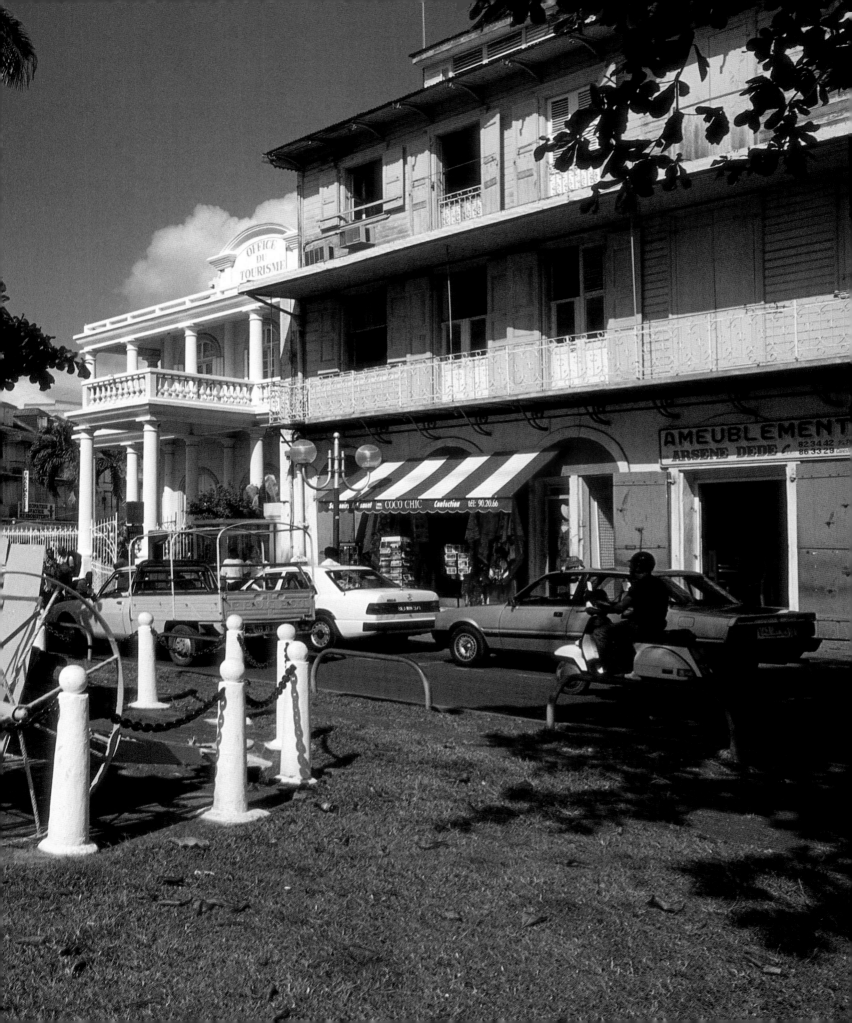

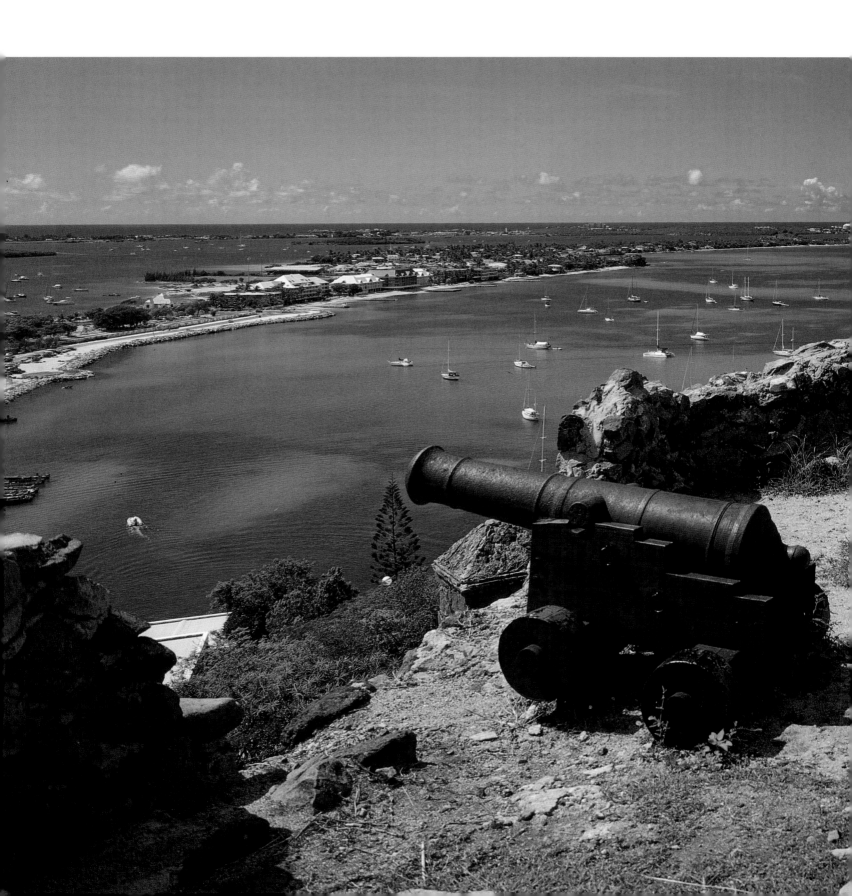

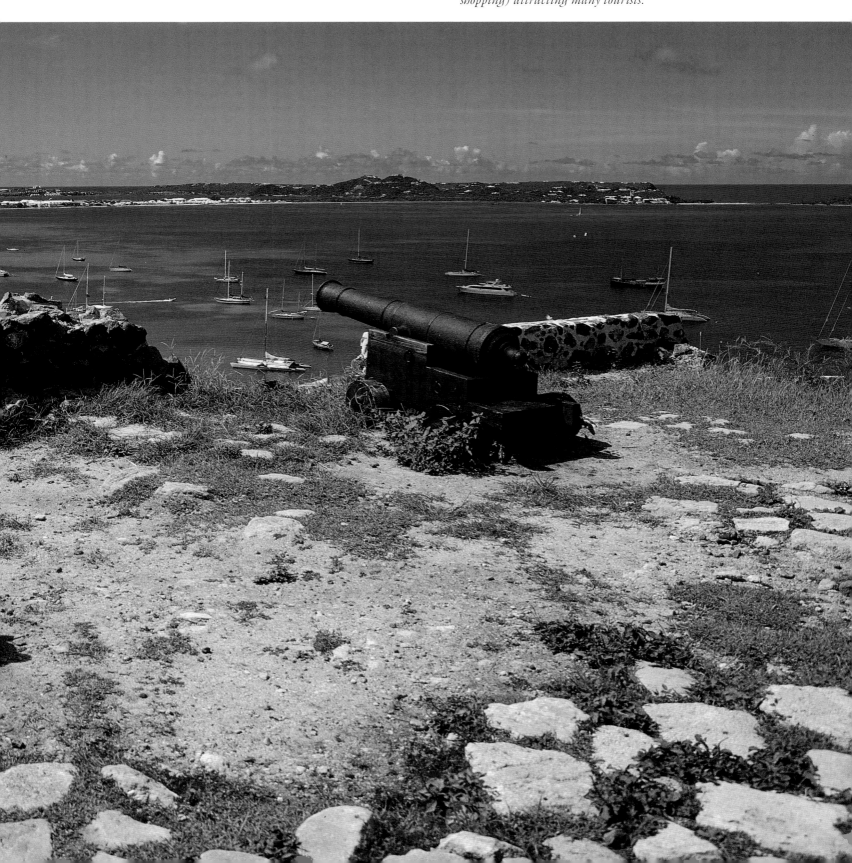

46-47 *On the island of St.Martin, the castle overlooking the town of Marigot offers a magnificent view of the whole bay. This island of the French Antilles is a much sought-after anchorage for cruise liners, its white-sand beaches, unspoilt coves and crystal-clear lagoons (as well as duty-free shopping) attracting many tourists.*

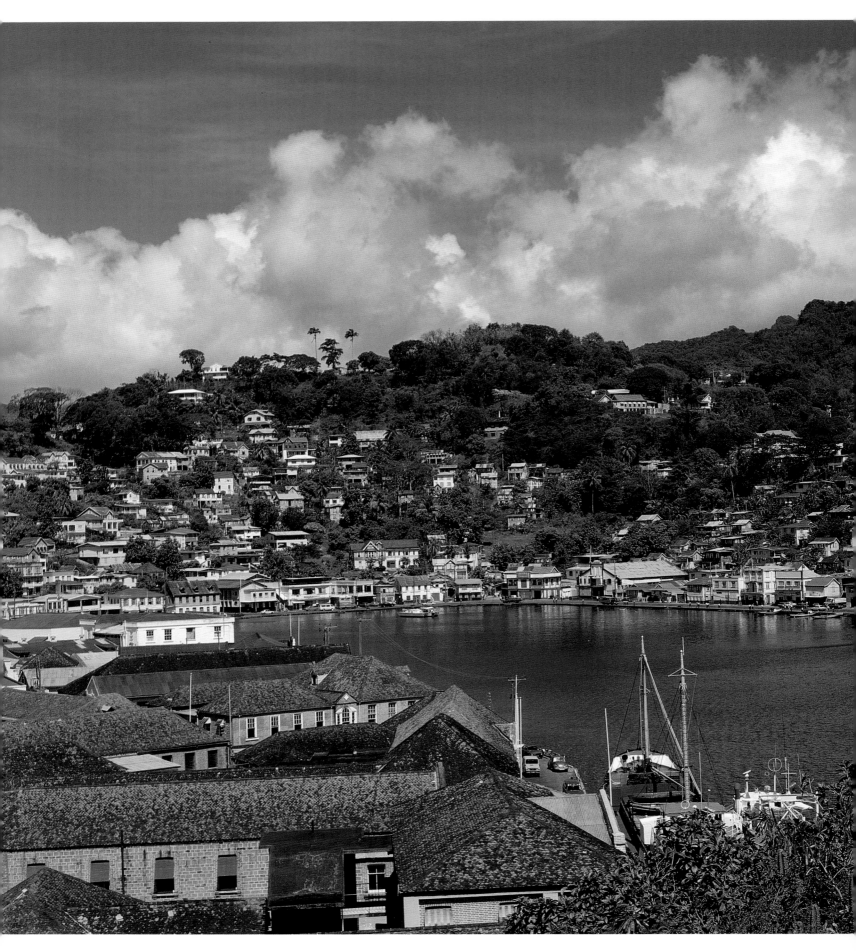

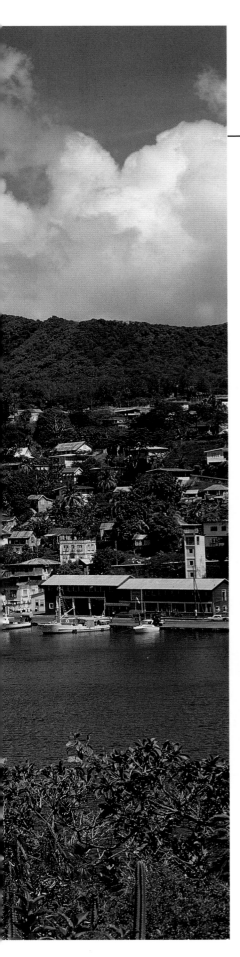

# St. Pierre,
# the Caribbean's own Pompei

48-49 *St.Pierre, the small port of Martinique, is known as the Pompei of the Caribbean: the town was completely destroyed in 1902 by a violent eruption of Montagne Pelée, which looms menacingly over it.*

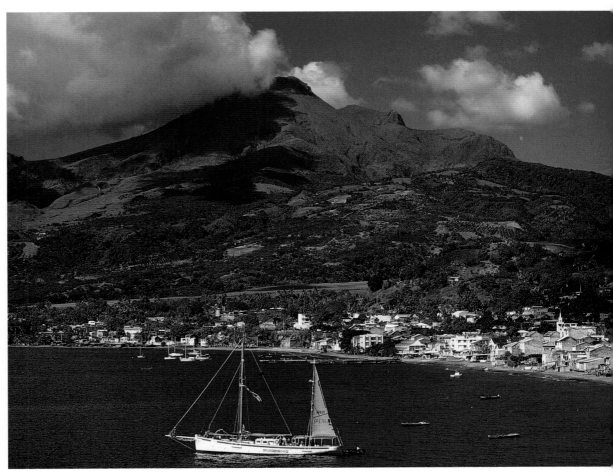

50-51 *Vessels of every kind - from sailing boats to luxury cruise ships - moor in the busy port of Charlotte Amalie, in the Virgin Islands.*

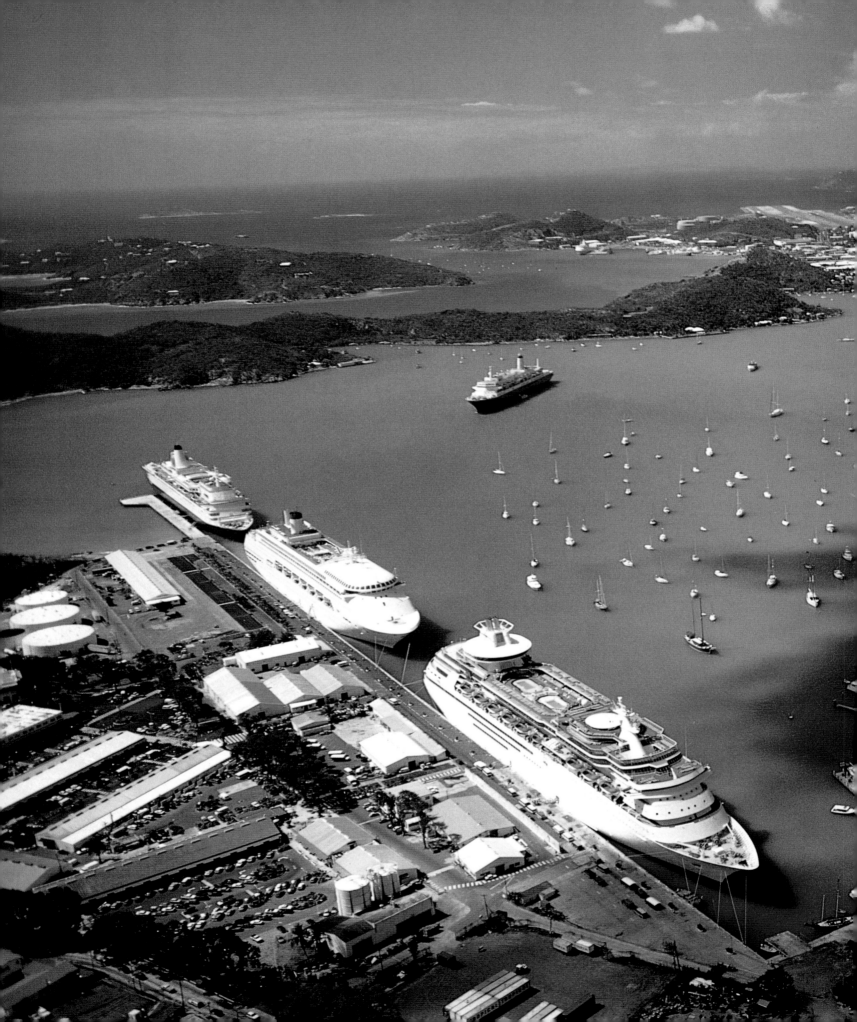

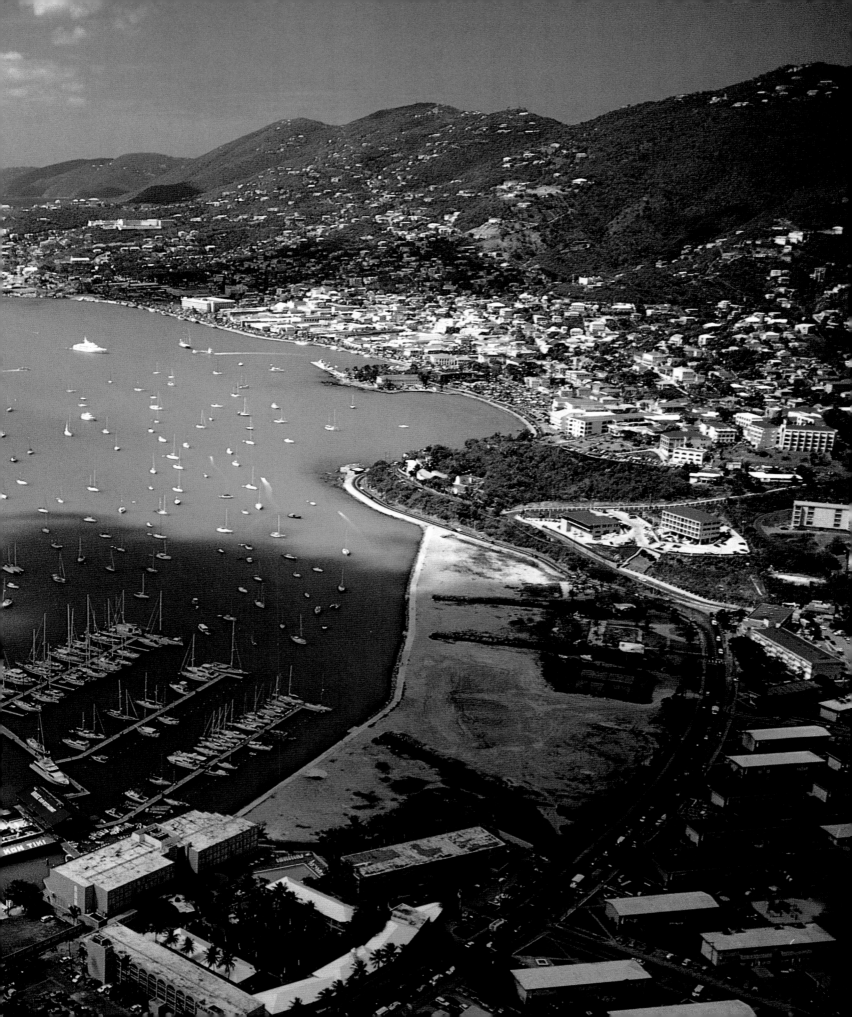

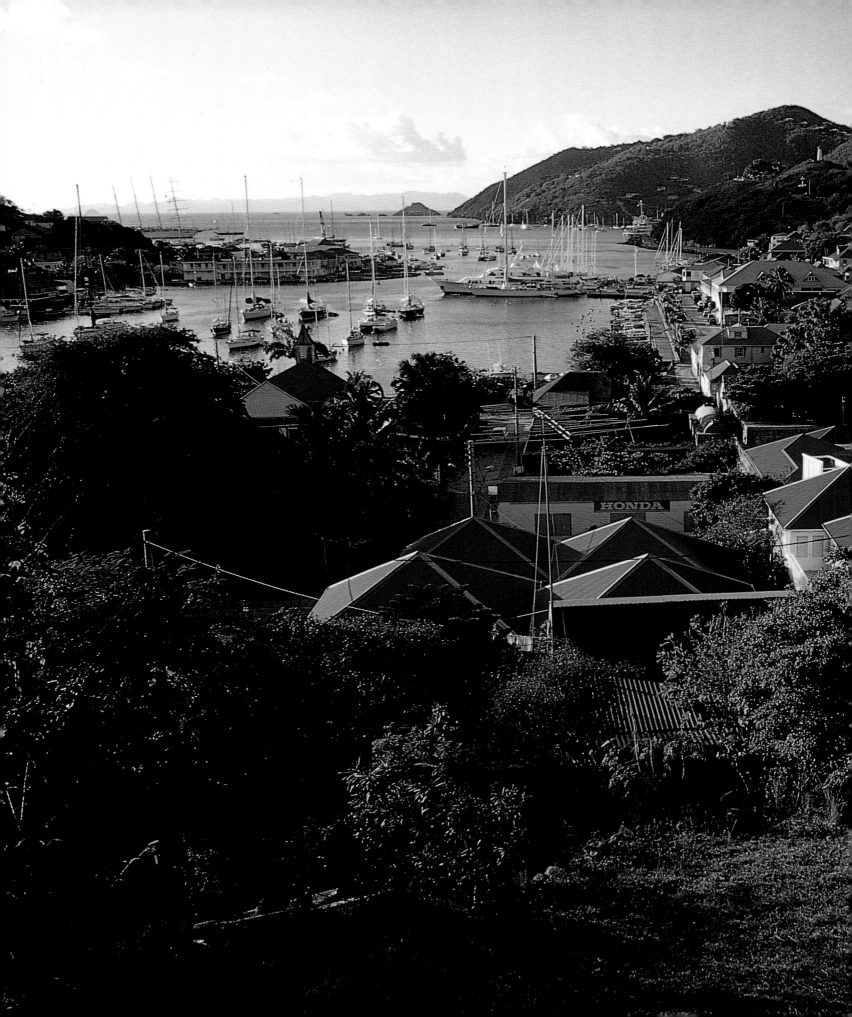

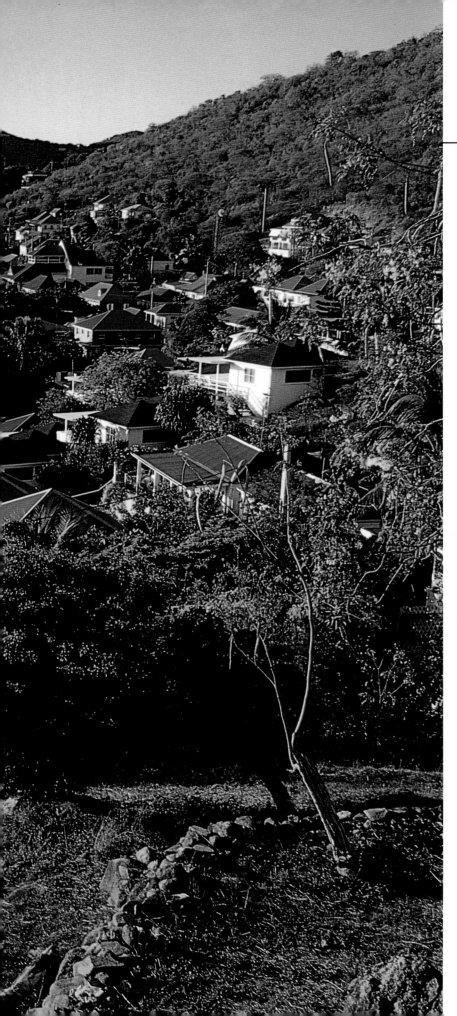

# Tropical sun,
# à la francaise

52-53 *The red roofs of Gustavia are a reminder of France's role in the settlement of St.Barthélemy. The town has a well-sheltered natural harbour, much frequented by an exclusive breed of tourists aboard luxury yachts.*

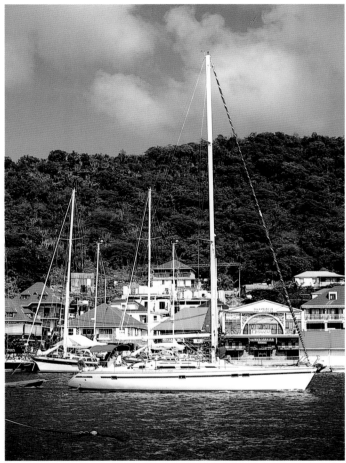

# From Ebony to Ivory

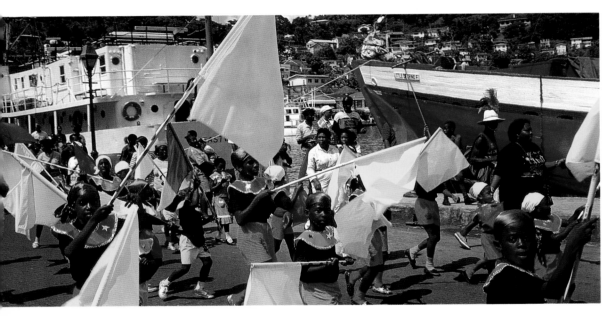

**54 top** *Waiting on the jetty to greet tourists arriving in Grenada is a carnival-style parade; dominating the scene are the vibrant colours typical of the Caribbean: grass green, golden yellow and coral red.*

**54 bottom** *The market at Pointe-à-Pitre invades the whole harbour area, even stretching along jetties where local people buy the daily catch straight from the fishing boats.*

**55** *The huge Saturday market brings a multi-coloured crowd to St.George's, capital town of Grenada, often to buy the home-grown spices for which the island is famous.*

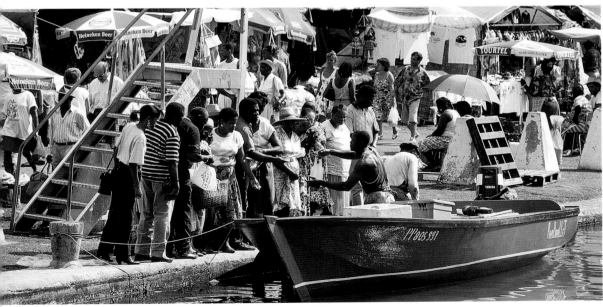

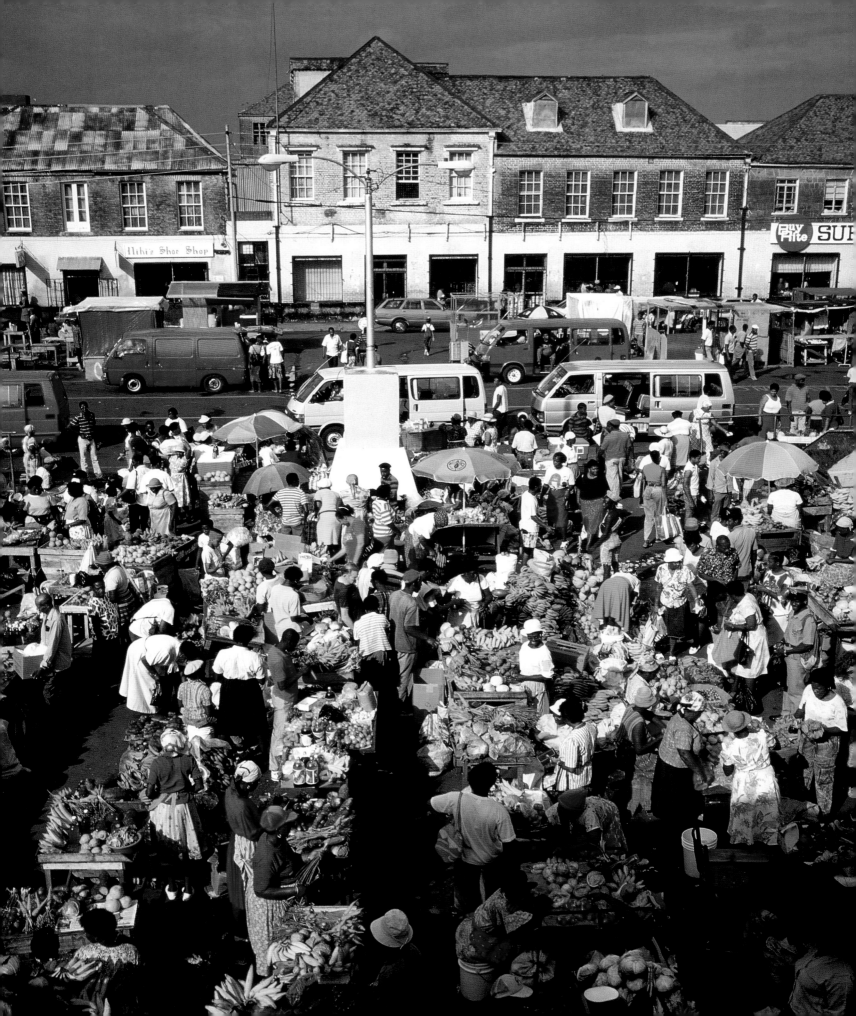

# Music and high spirits to the tempo of the Tropics

56 *Any time of day is right for music and frenetic dancing, while tourists look on in envy and amazement.*

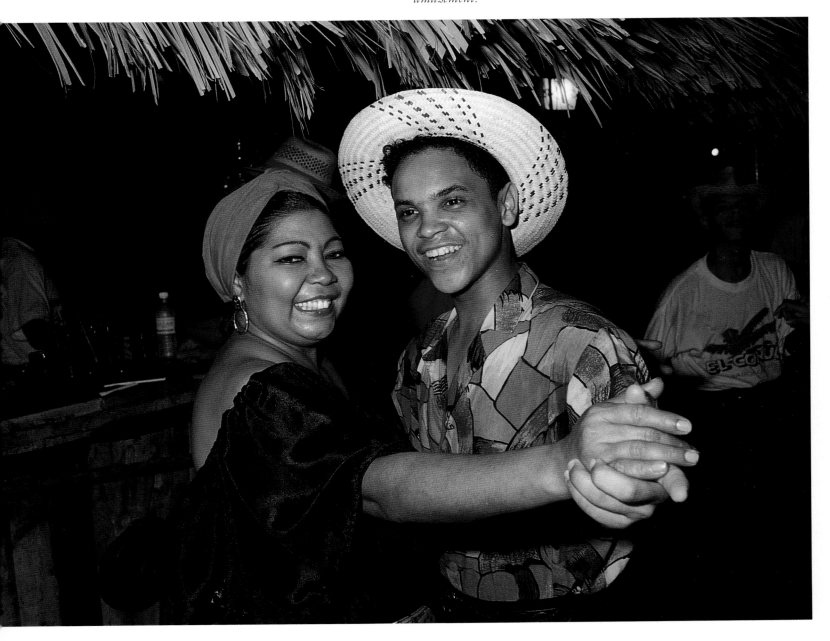

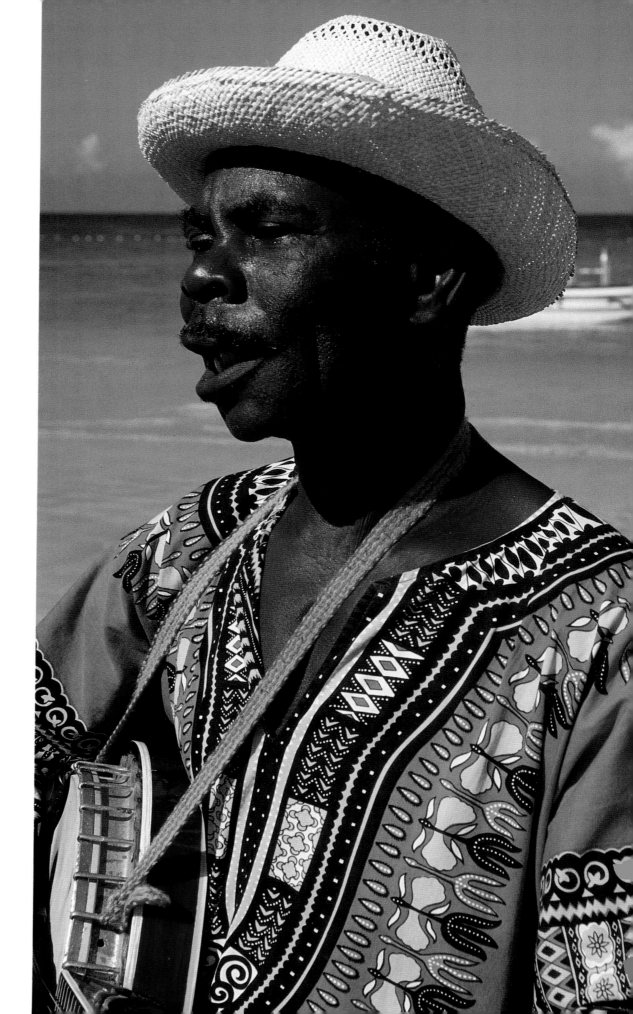

57 *Straw hats and gaudily-printed shirts give a colourful, picturesque look to even the most ordinary Caribbean islander.*

58-59 *Against the fascinating backdrop of the Tropics natural beauty and local beauties vie for attention.*

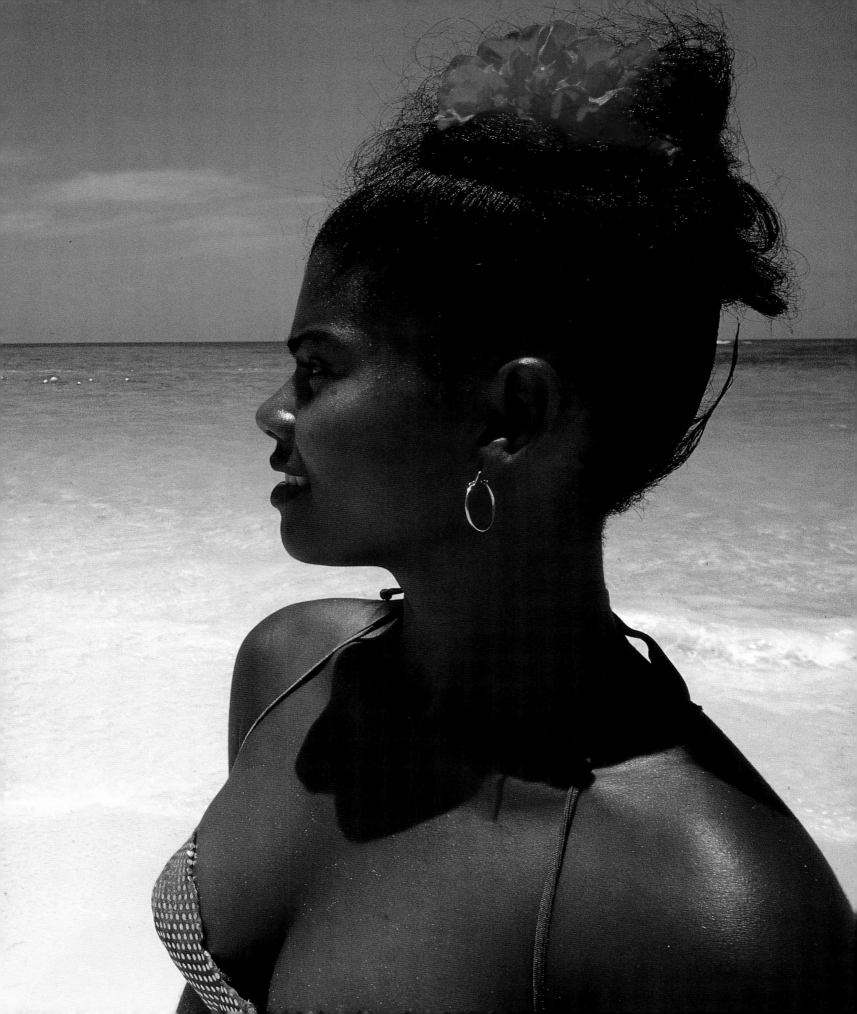

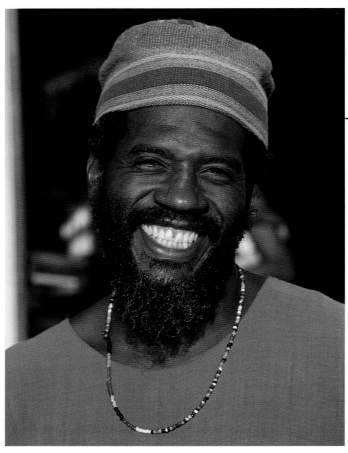

# Martinique and Guadeloupe: sun, sea and ... Creole culture

60-61 *Martinique and Guadeloupe are citadels of what could be called Gallic-style Creole language and culture. The Afro hairstyles of men and women in Pointe-à-Pitre and of this delightful little girl, pictured elsewhere in the French Antilles, point to the strong link still existing between the continent of Africa and the islands of the Caribbean.*

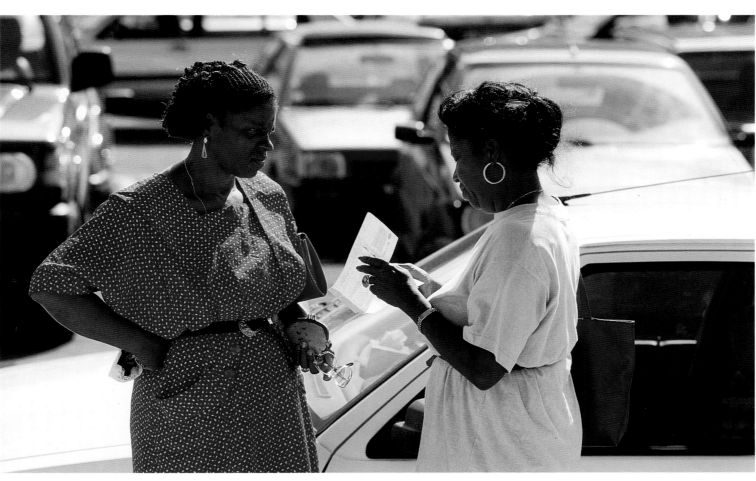

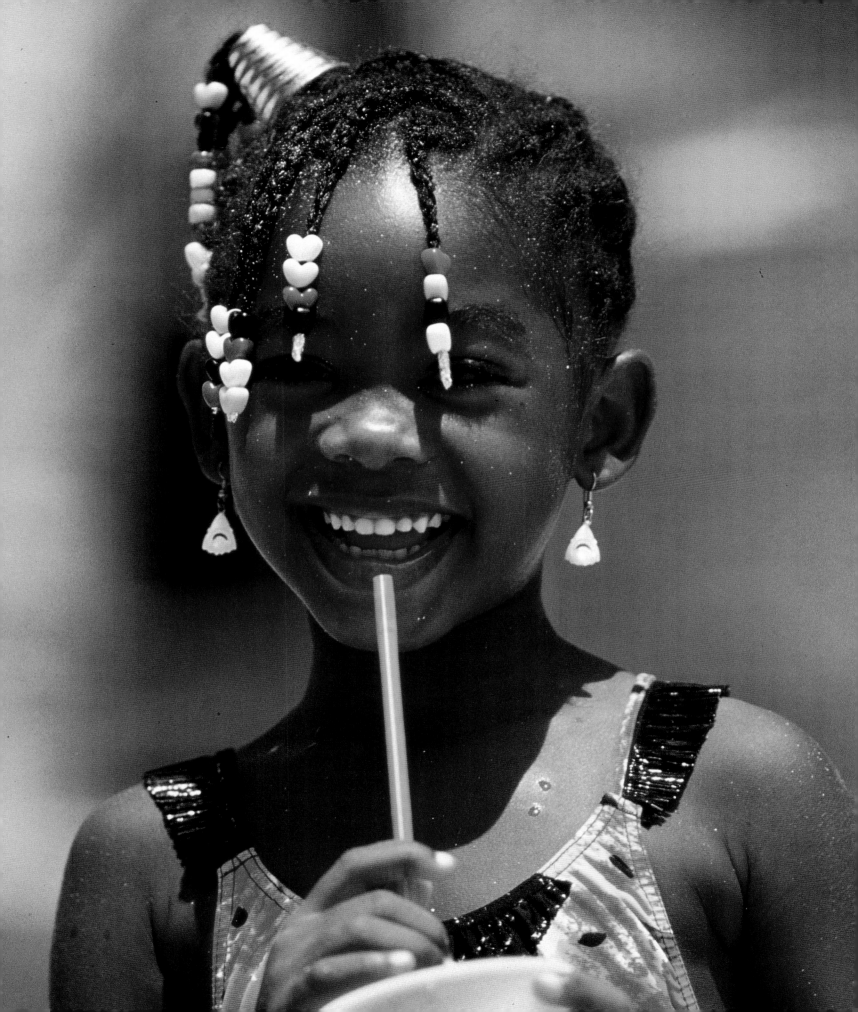

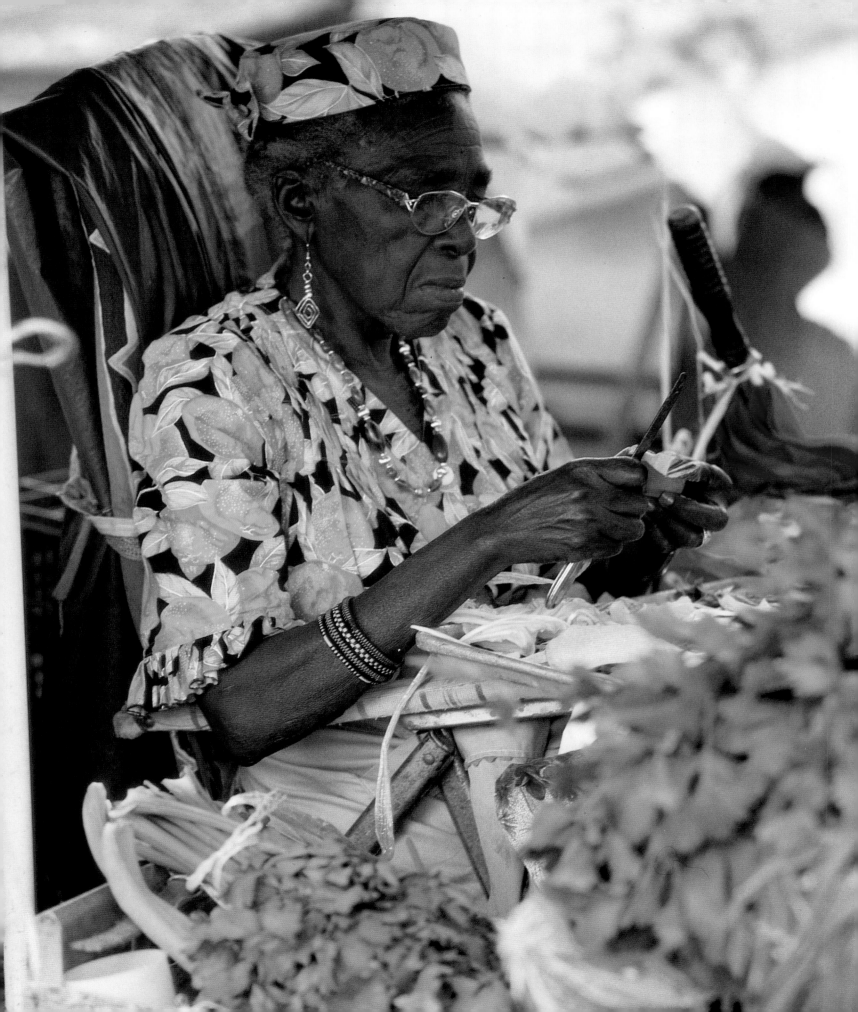

62-63  *Poverty and plenty come together at the market in Basse-Terre, second-largest town of Guadeloupe. Patched-up sunshades, makeshift stalls and pieces of cloth spread on the ground are used to display the merchandise: a splendid assortment of island produce - fruit, vegetables, spices and flour.*

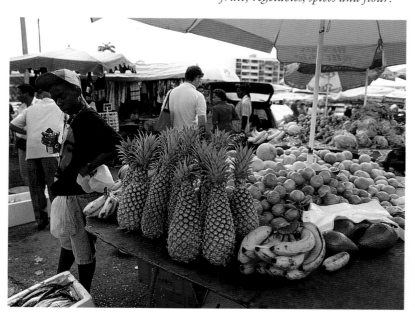

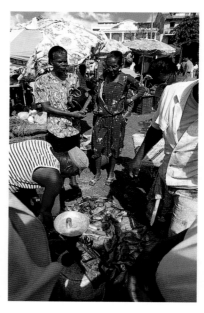

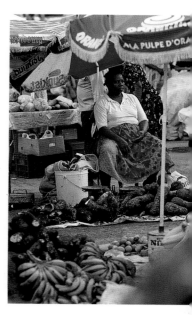

64-65  *Along these volcanic beaches of grey sand, traditional fishing methods are still in use today.*

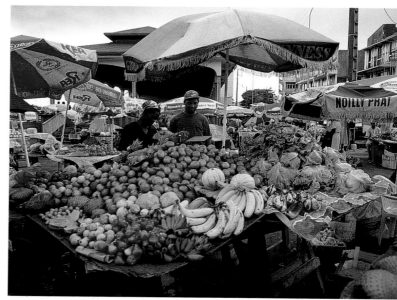

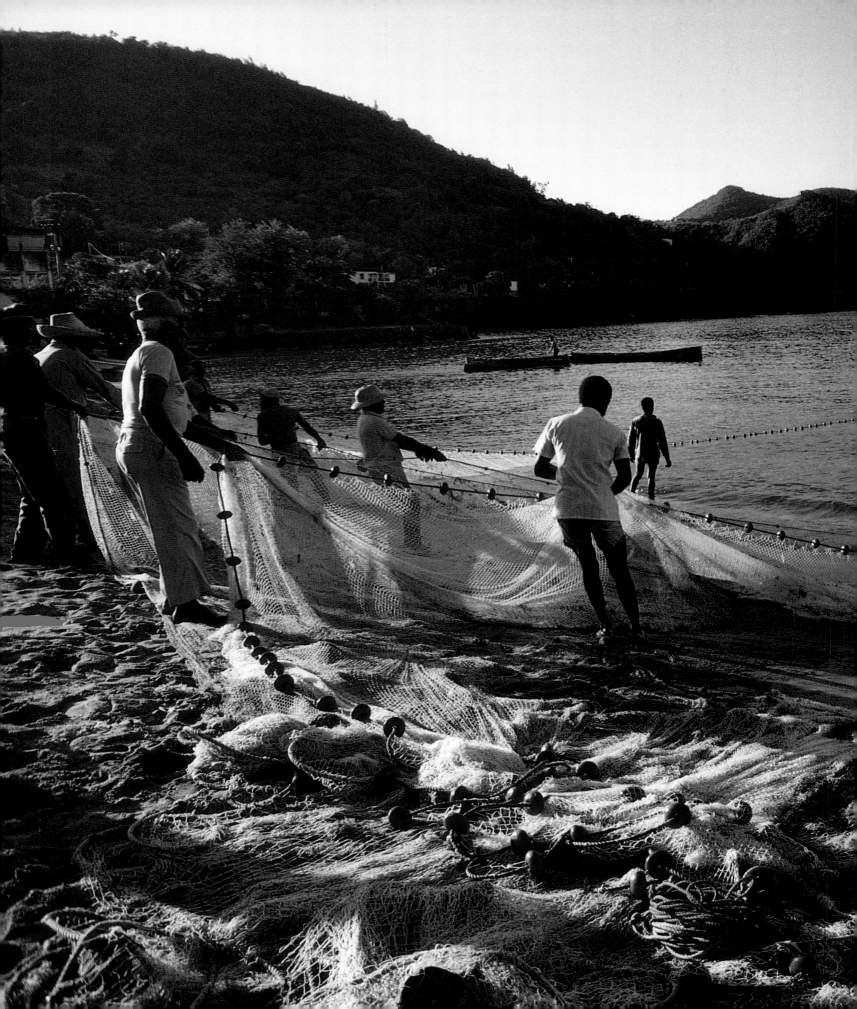

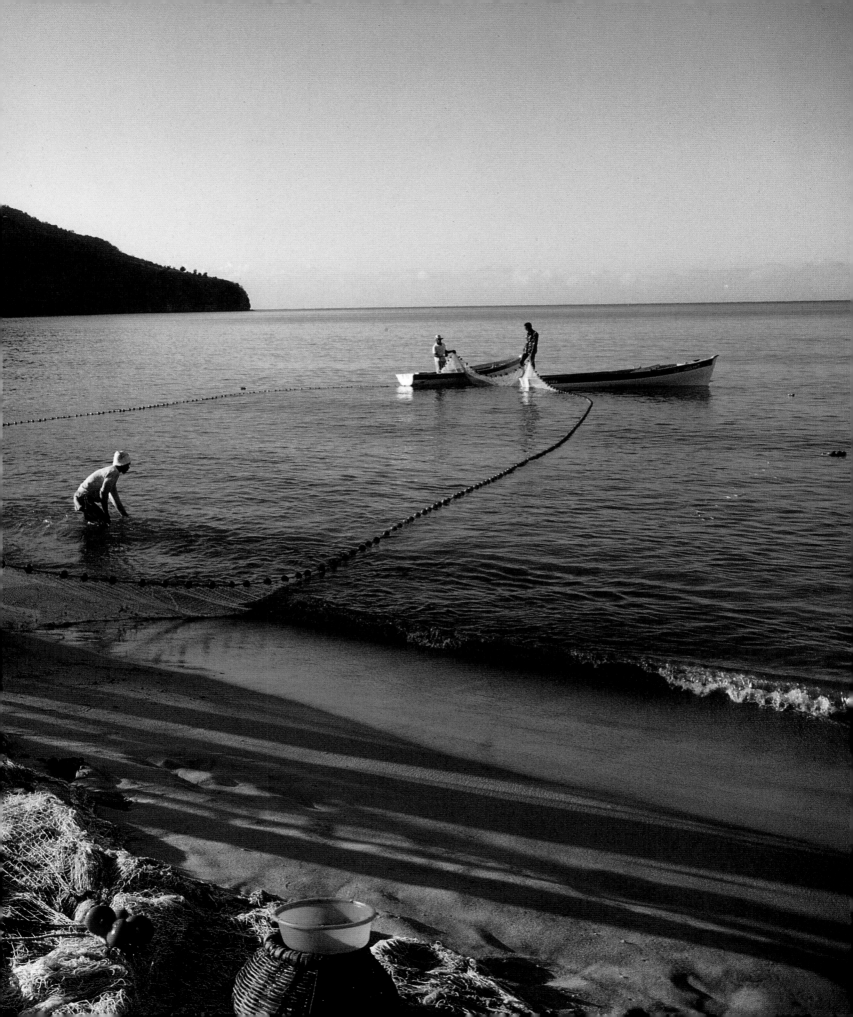

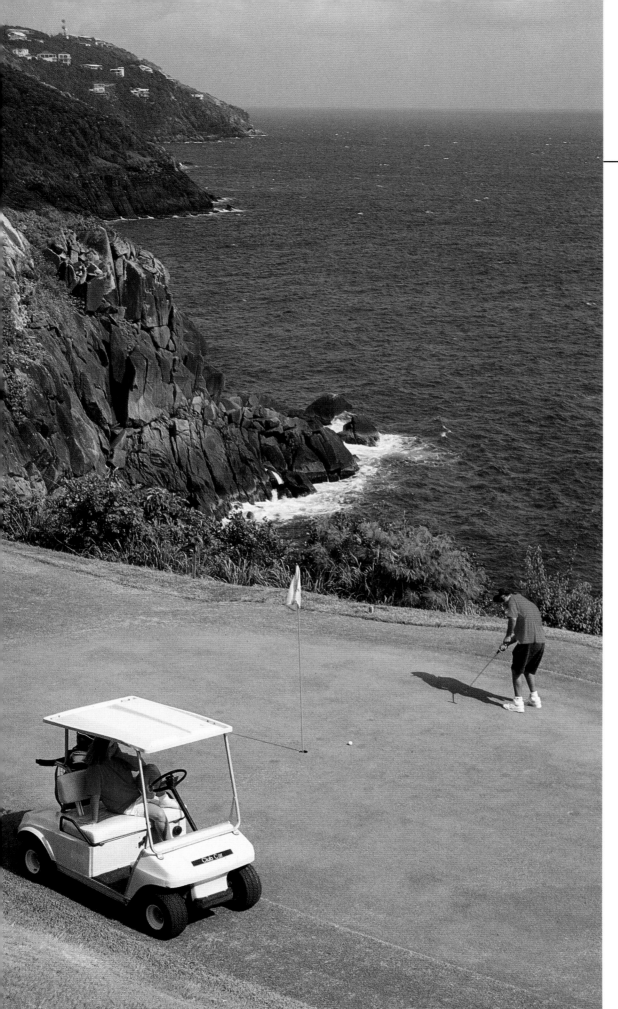

# Sport and relaxation beneath the Caribbean sun

66  *Countless facets of modern Western life-styles have now "colonized" the Caribbean islands. The passion for golf, imported from Britain and America, has led to the development of some amazing golf courses clinging to rocky clifftops.*

67  *Bathed in the golden light of the setting sun is Salines Beach, one of the few beaches of Martinique with white sand.*

68-69  *The French Antilles are a favourite destination for sailing enthusiasts: rain and clouds are a rarity and there are plenty of sheltered coves and inlets in which to cast anchor.*

70-71  *The turquoise blue water of the pool, an aquamarine sea, breezes gently moving the fronds of the palm trees: seen from the Hotel Manapani, St.Barthélemy is every holidaymaker's dream.*

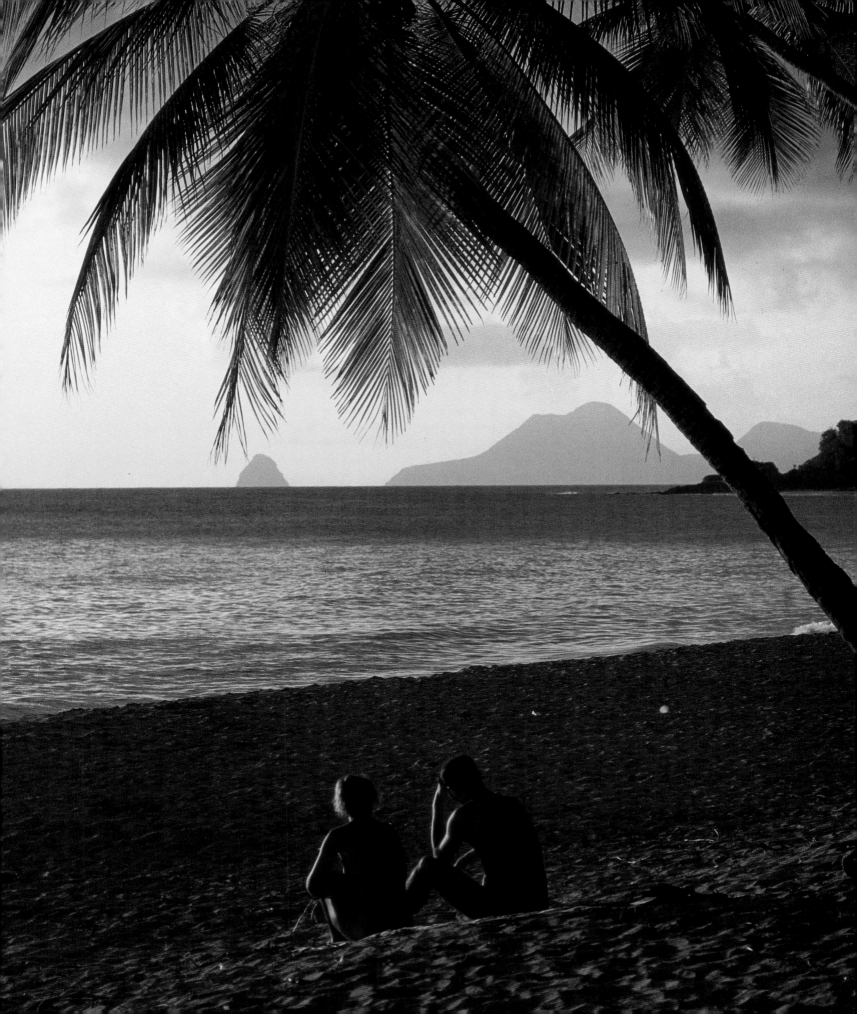

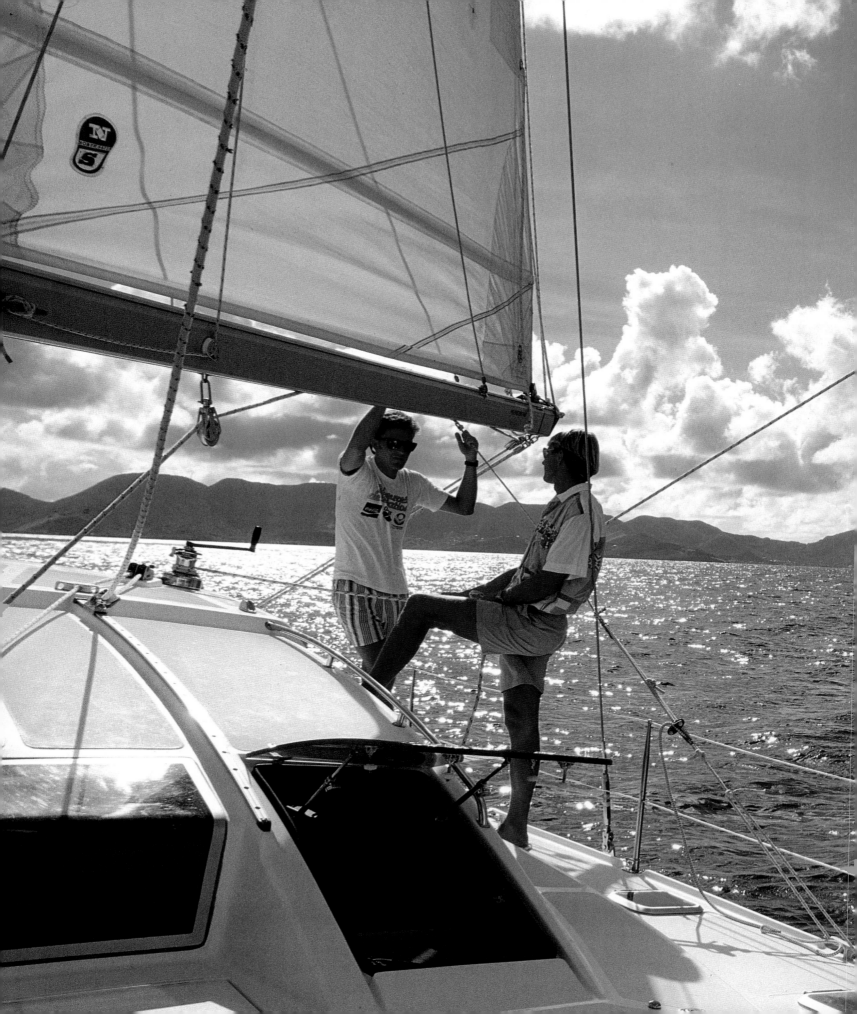

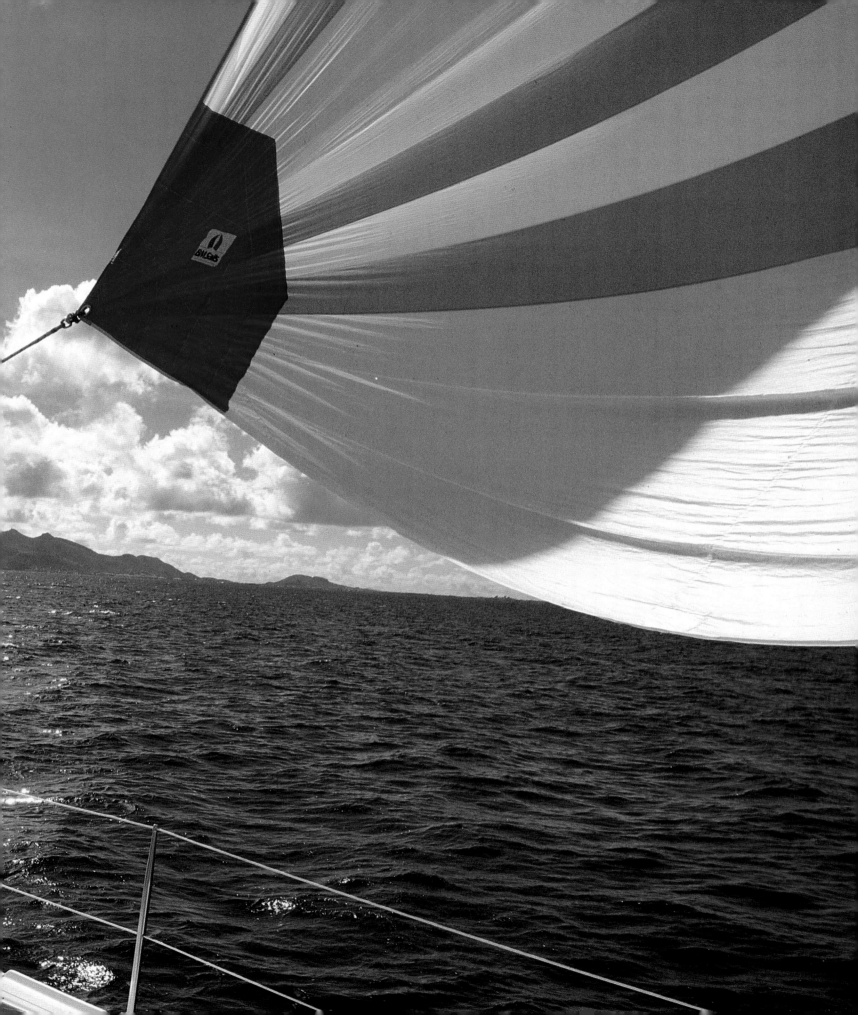

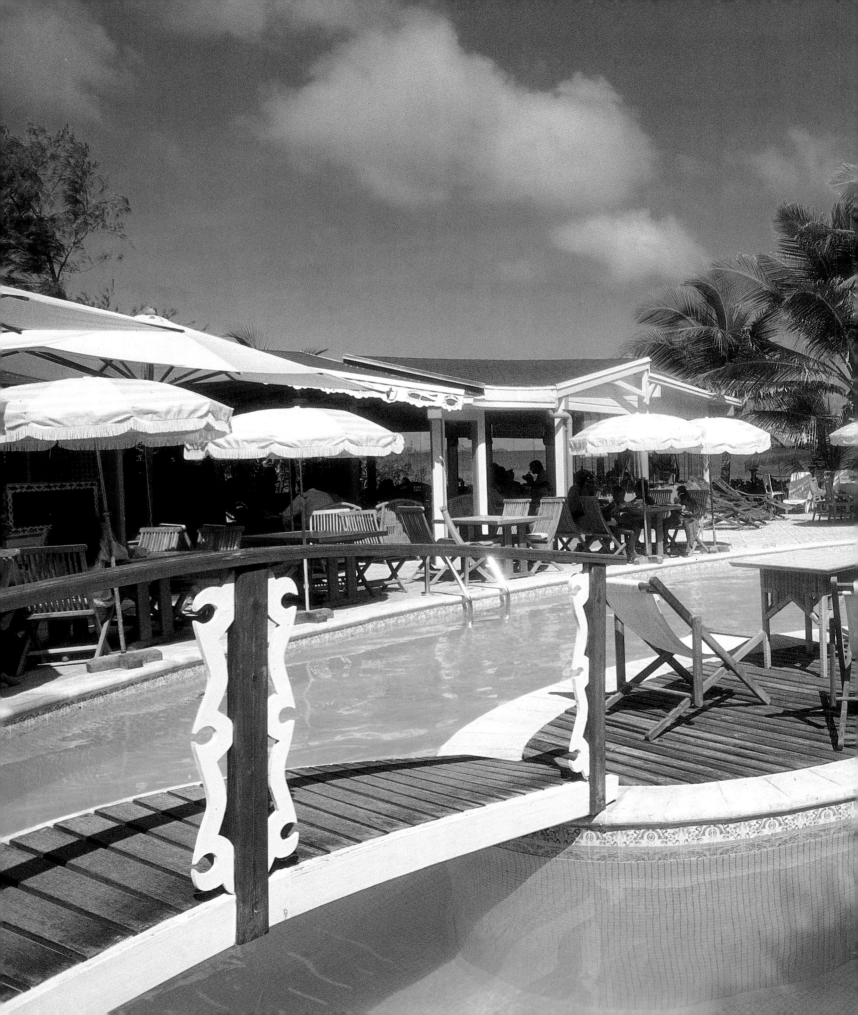

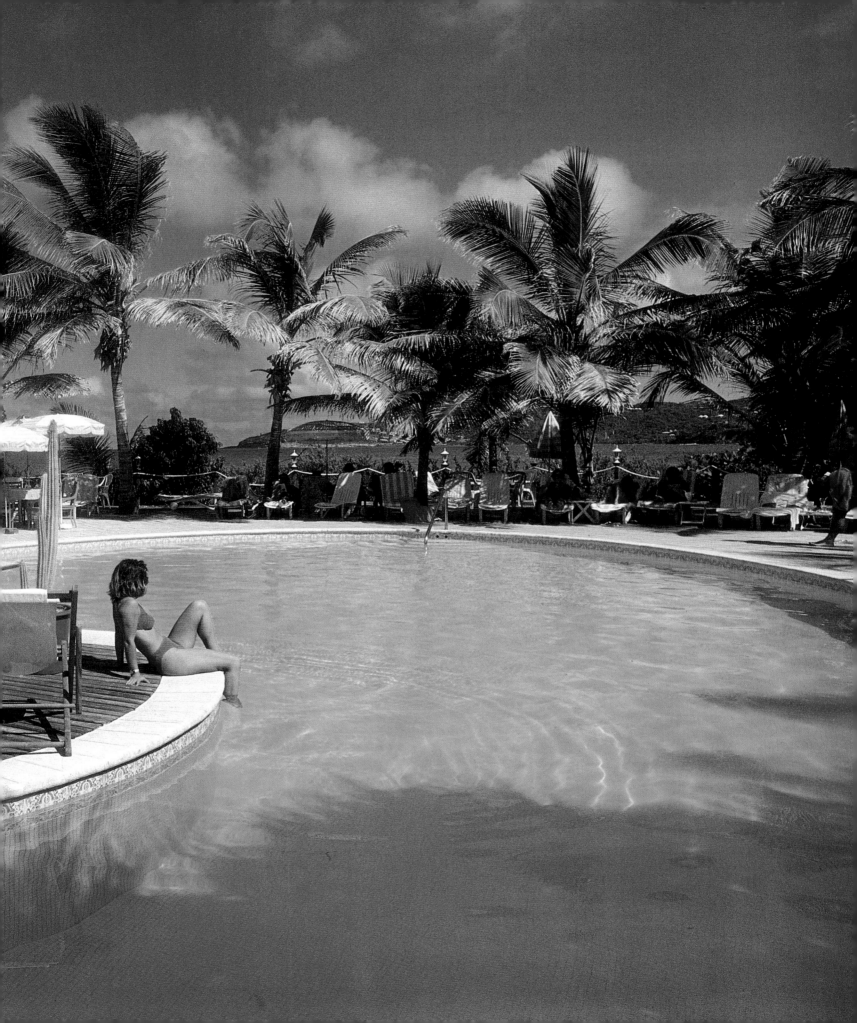

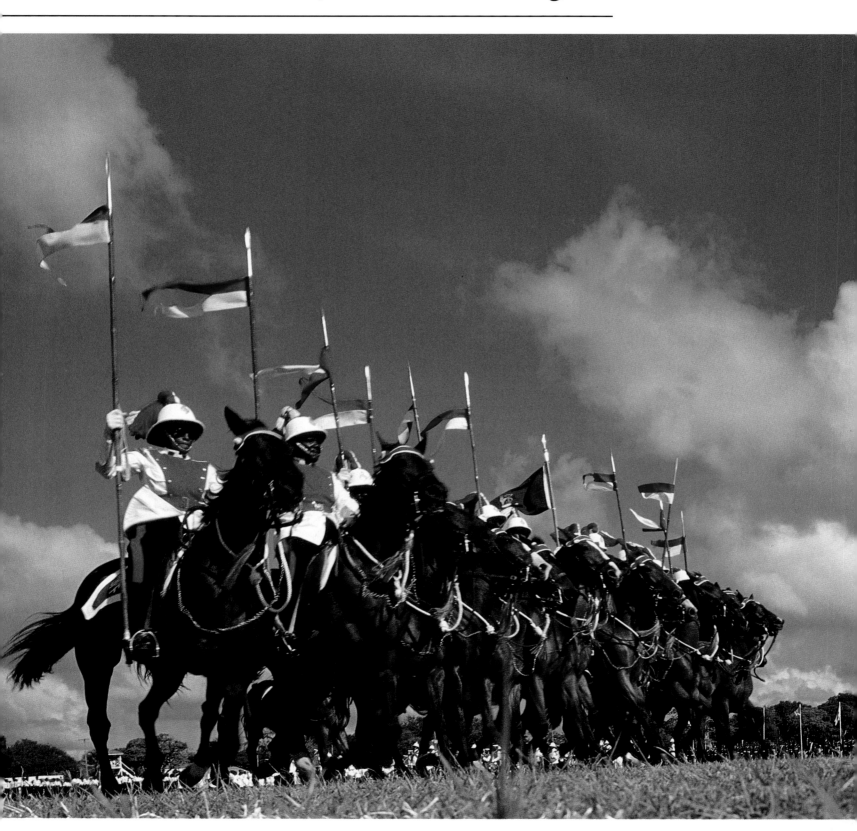

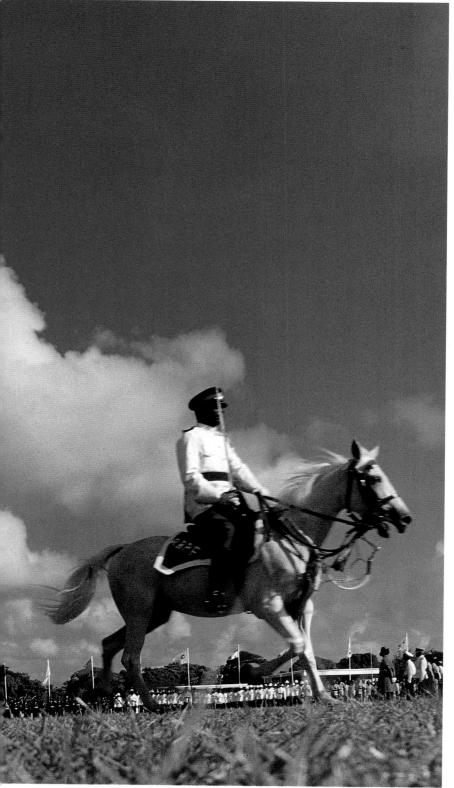

72-73 In Bridgetown, capital of Barbados, Independence Day is celebrated with a traditional parade which, although an essentially formal event, has plenty of Caribbean charm. A British colony since 1625, the island became independent in 1966; it is now a member of the British Commonwealth.

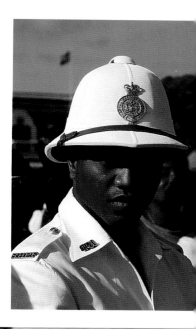

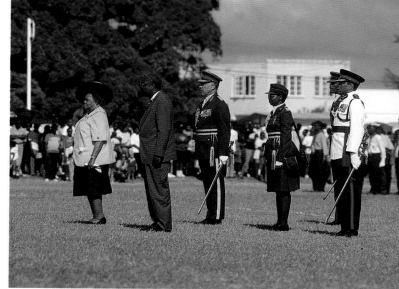

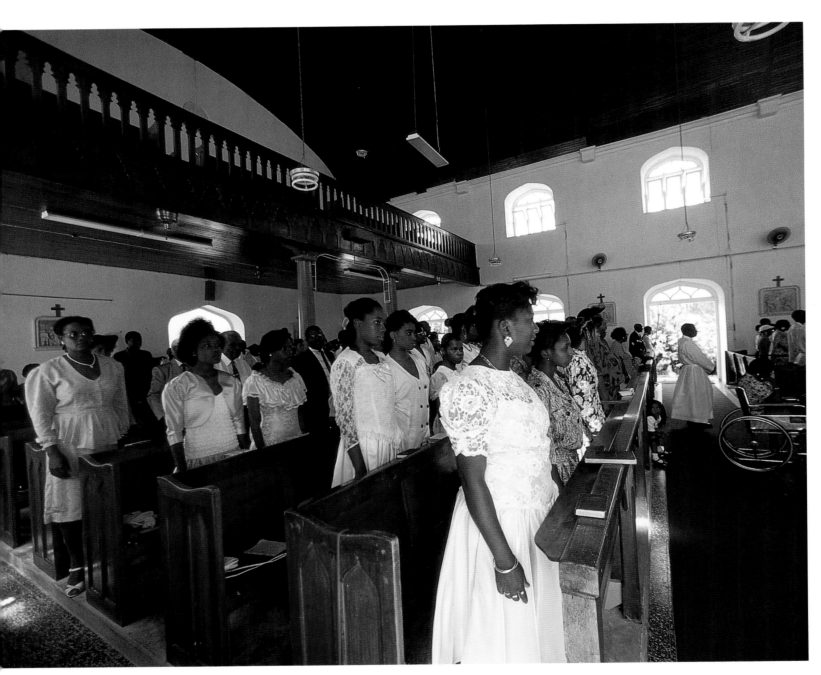

74  *A few miles from the capital of Barbados is Oistins, the town where the 'Barbados Charter' establishing British rule was signed in 1625. Oistins has a large religious community, as can be seen from the many people in this congregation attending Sunday service.*

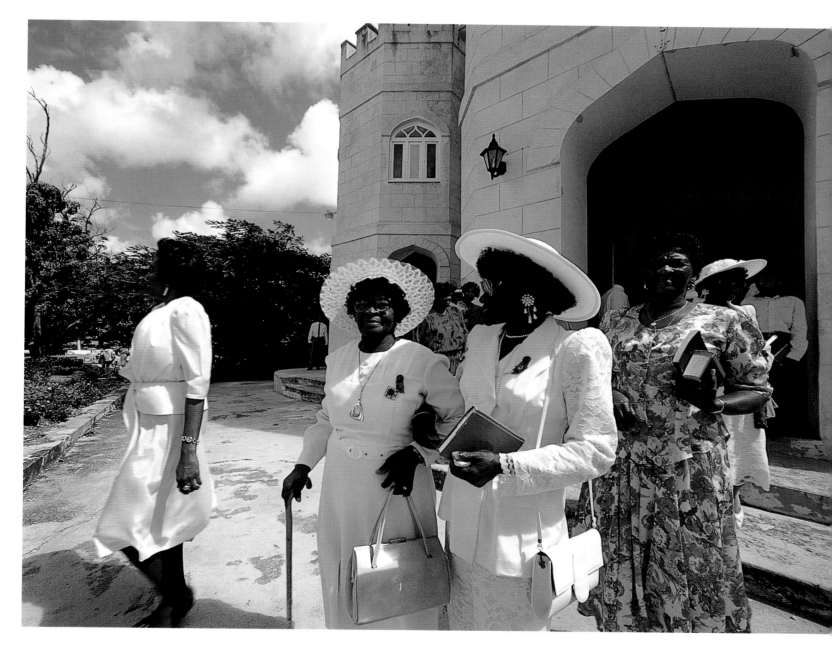

75 *Western dress and indigenous attire are equally in vogue among churchgoers. In the graveyard adjoining Oistins church is a crypt called Mystery Vault, said to be haunted by ghosts.*

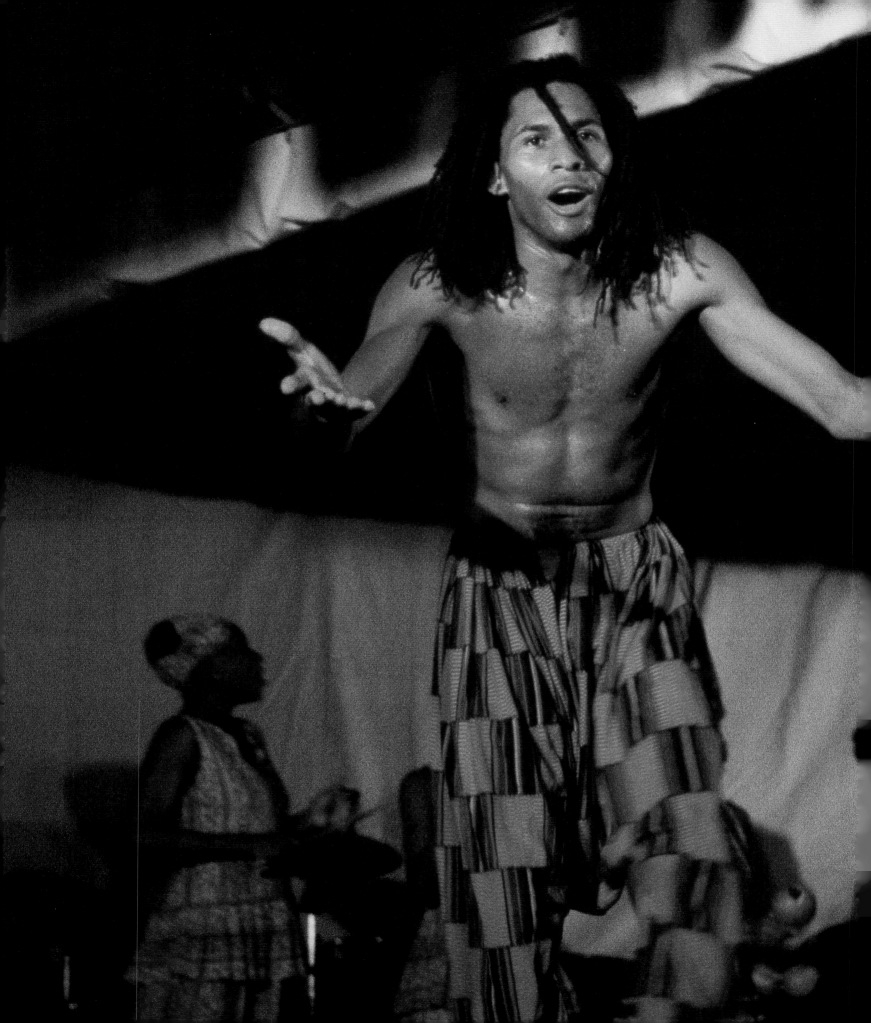

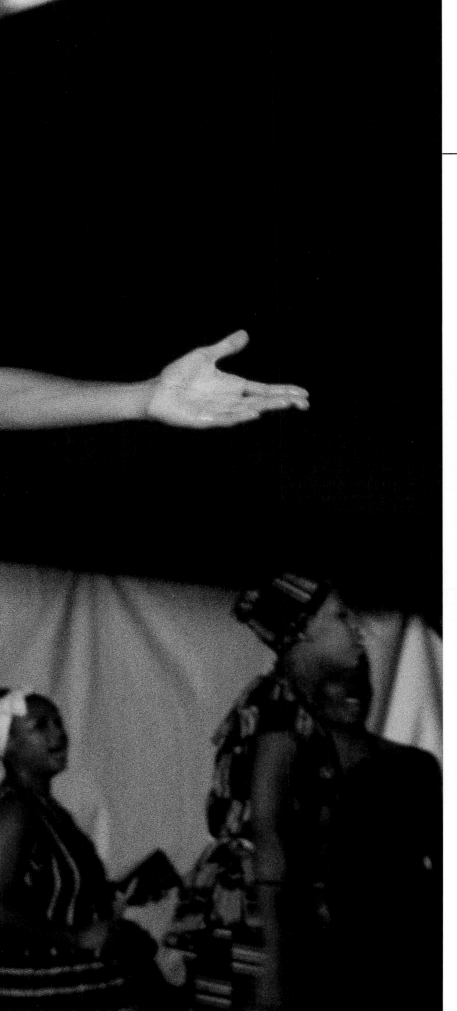

# Island with an African heart

76-77  *African music and dancing is very much alive in the 'melting-pot' culture of the Caribbean islands to which Africa, Europe and Asia have contributed through the centuries.*

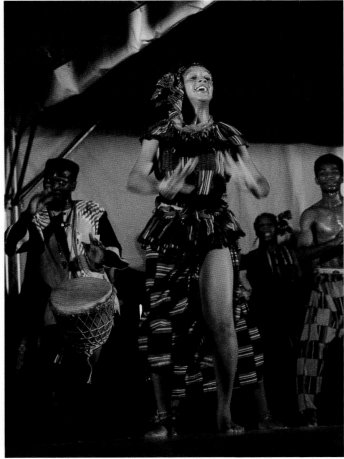

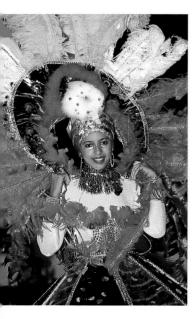

78-79 *The colourful and flamboyant masked carnival held in Grenada, southernmost of the Windward Islands, owes much to Creole folklore, a mixture of European and African religious beliefs. By far the largest ethnic group on the island is of Central African origin: 80% of its 100,000 inhabitants are black, 15% of mixed descent and only 5% white.*

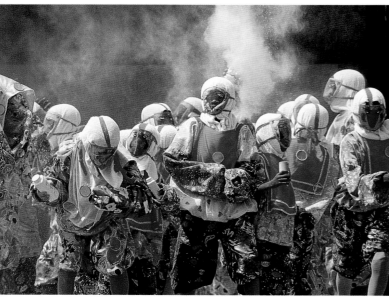

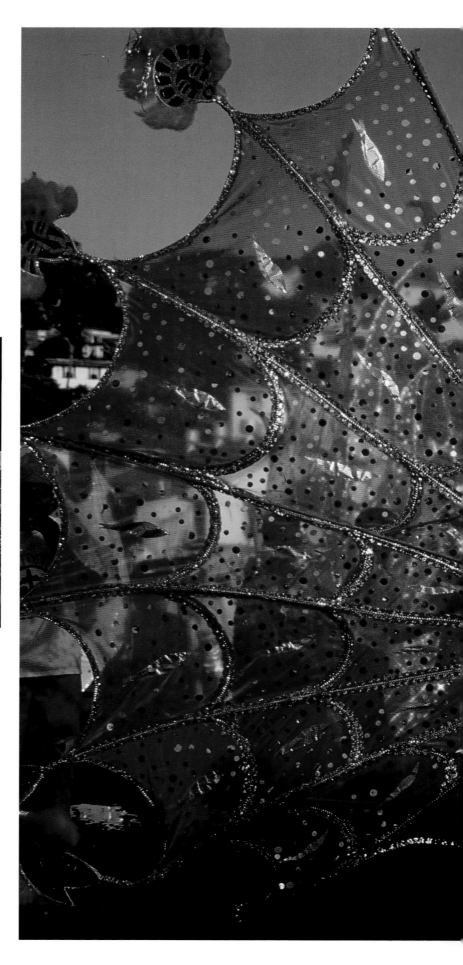

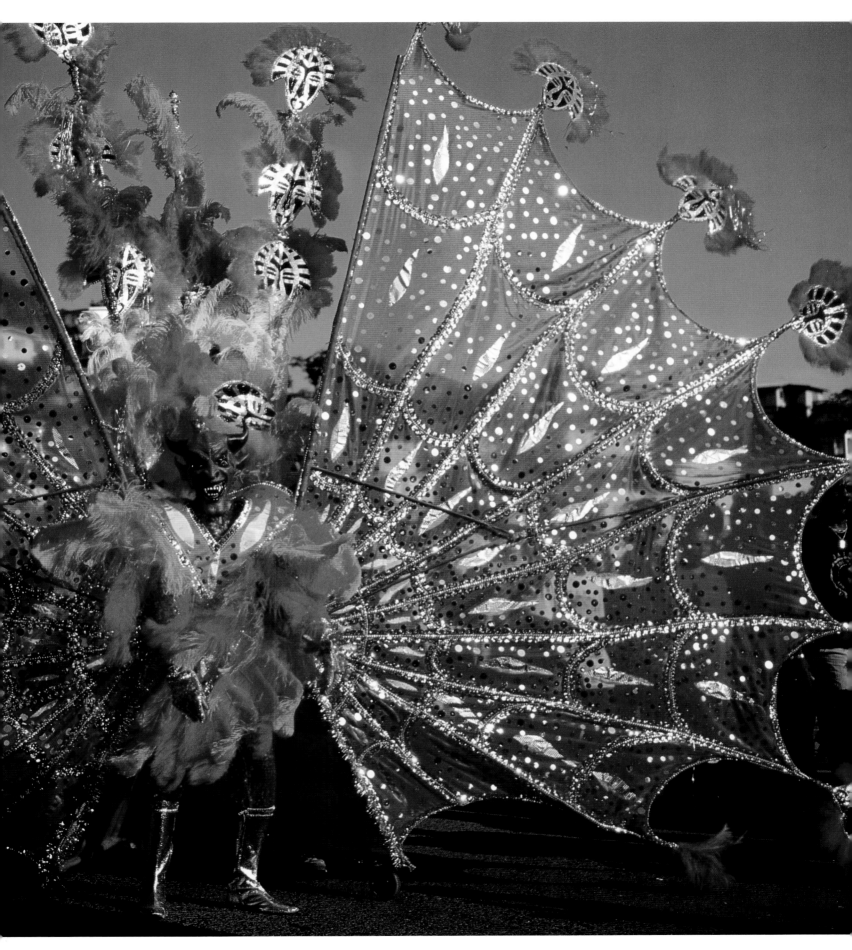

# Earth's Last Eden

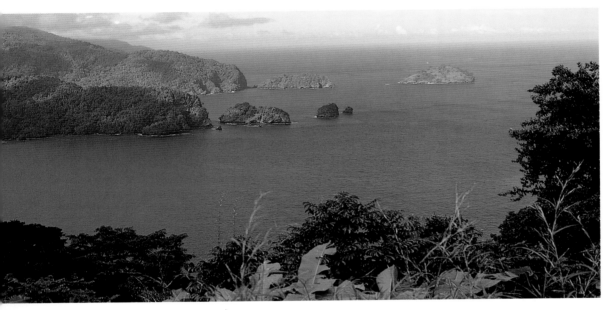

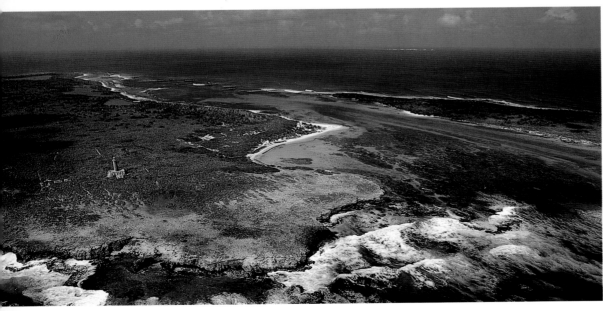

80 top *Swept by the Trade Winds, with a shore on which lush vegetation stretches towards a stunningly blue sea, La Vache bay is one of the most beautiful spots on the island of Trinidad.*

80 bottom *At some distance from Guadeloupe, facing the promontory of Pointe des Chateaux, the tiny islands of Petite-Terre offer unspoiled nature.*

81 *White sand and deep blue ocean, fringed by tall palms and by the coral reef just offshore, the beach of Las Cuevas Bay in Trinidad is a sight that reflects most people's idea of paradise.*

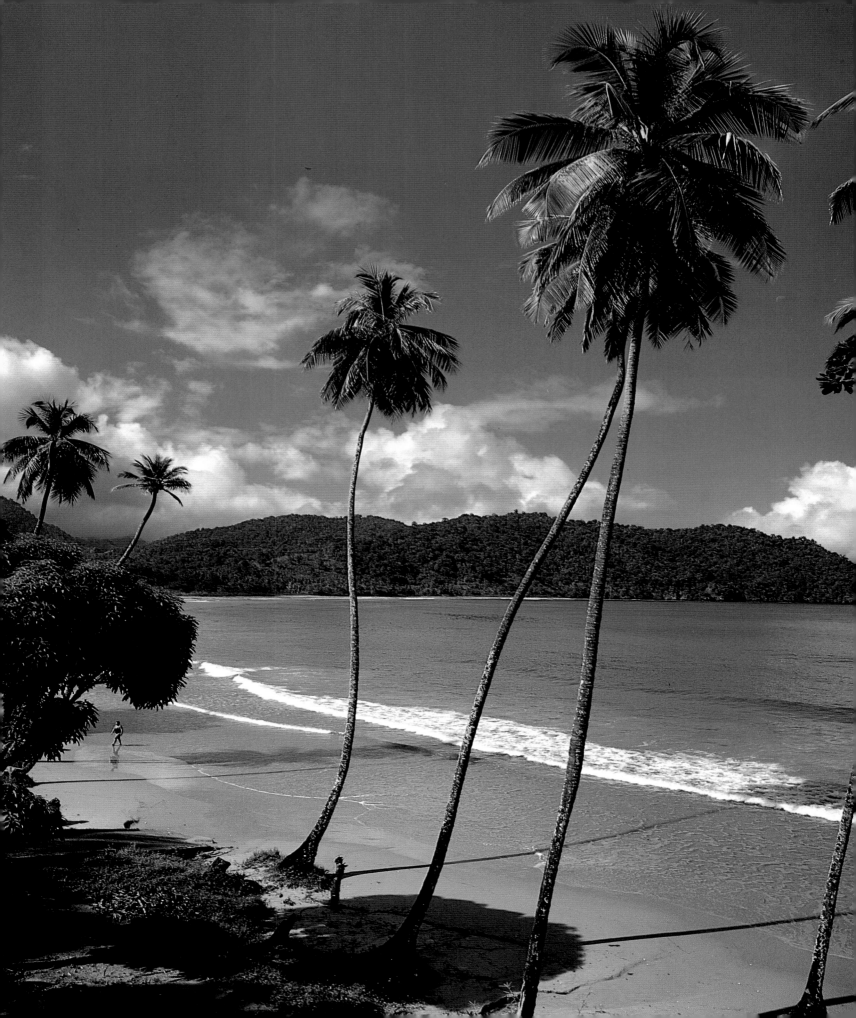

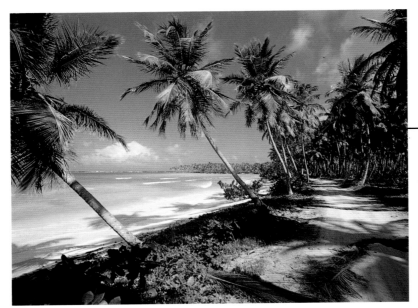

# The heavenly beaches of paradise on Earth

*82 top  Wind-bent palm trees overhang one of the delightful beaches south of Punta Cana, in the vicinity of the Bavaro Hotel, in Santo Domingo, in the Dominican Republic.*

*82 bottom  Facing Isla Saona, in Santo Domingo, is the glorious shady beach of Ventaglio Club Dominicus resort hotel.*

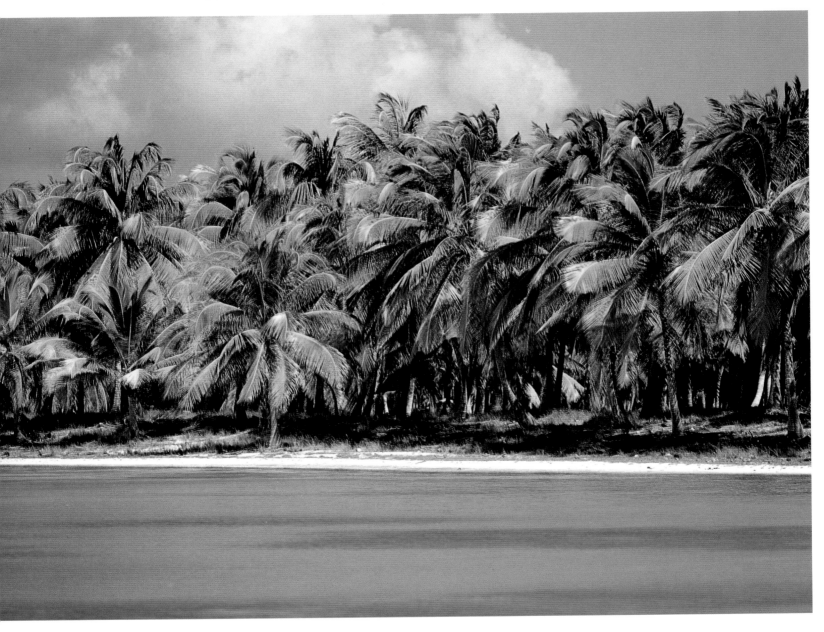

83 *The rainbow colours of sailing boats moored at Punta Cana, a smart resort close to Santo Domingo, are reflected in the turquoise blue waters.*

84-85 *Set in the deep blue of the Caribbean is the small Isla Saona, an unspoilt island of the Dominican Republic just off its southern shores.*

86-87 *The splendour of Jamaica's northern coast is revealed in this picture taken near Port Antonio, a small town with a magnificent and well-sheltered double harbour.*

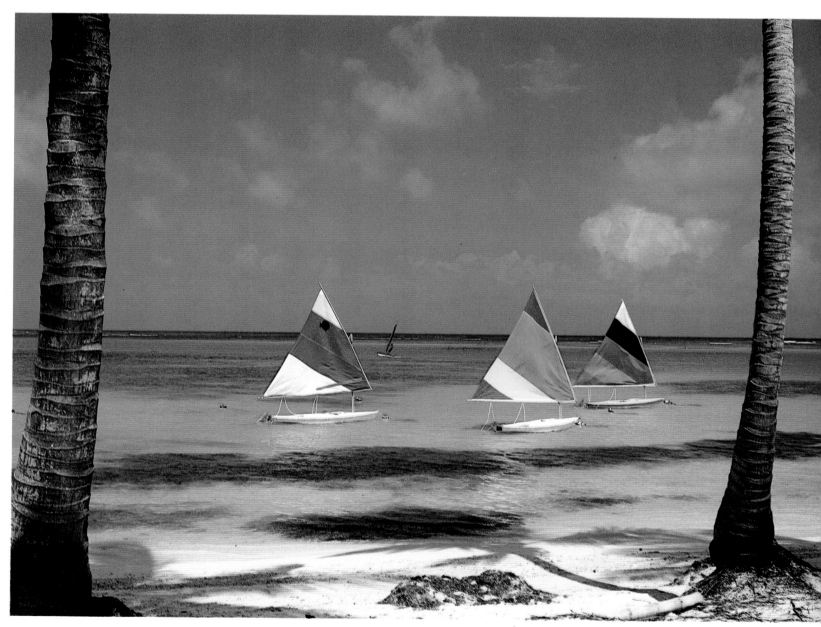

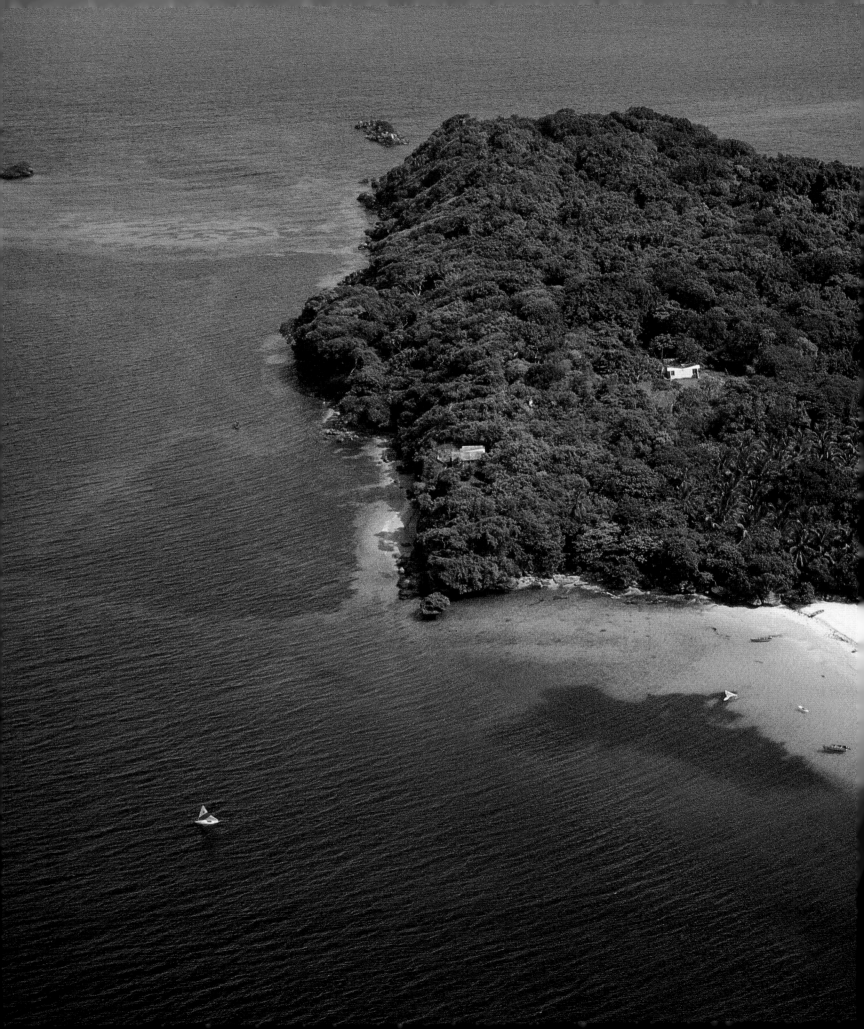

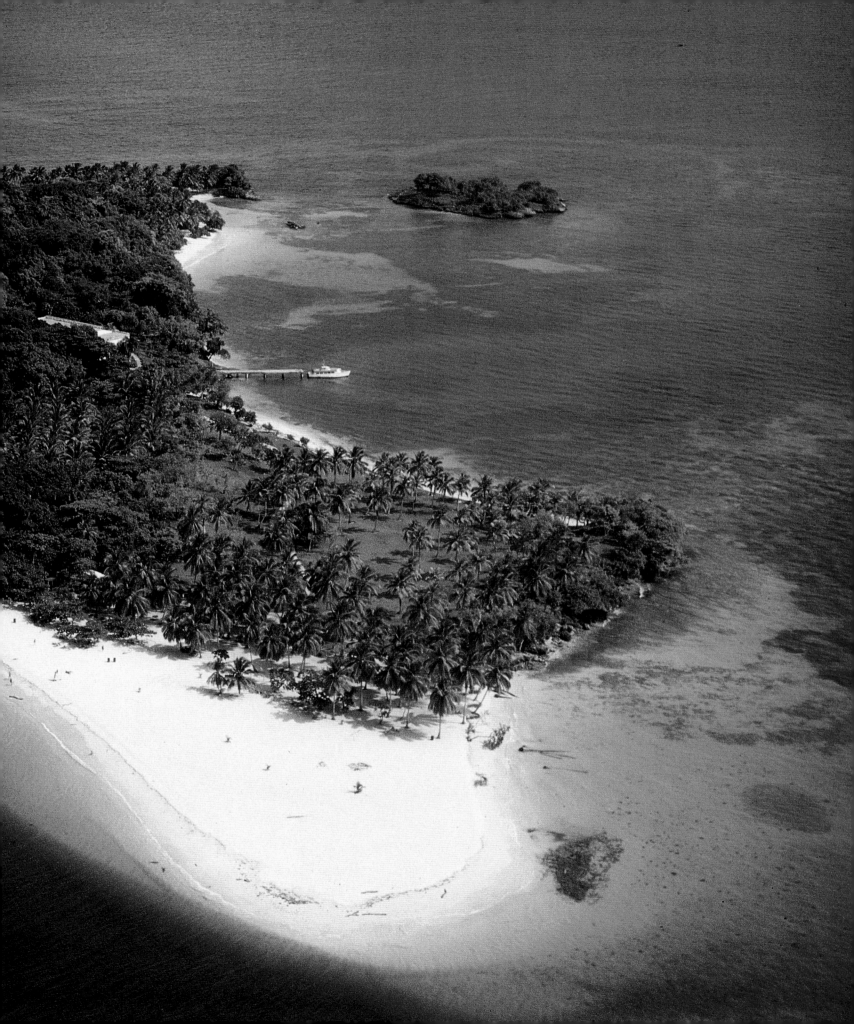

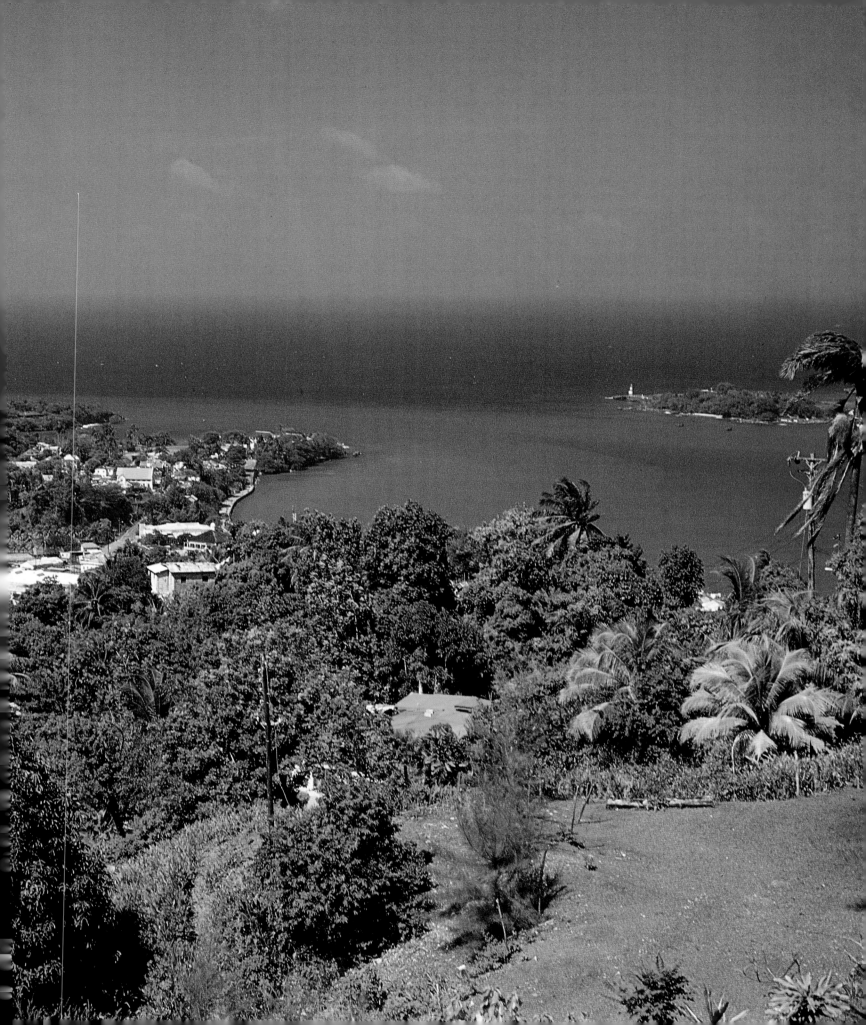

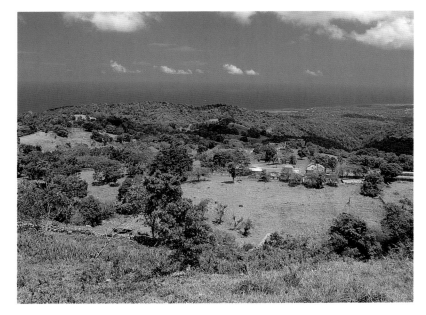

88 top *The countryside inland from Ocho Rios, a popular resort town, has some of the loveliest scenery in Jamaica and trekking on horseback is an ideal way to explore.*

88 bottom *With pools of blue-green water rimmed with rocks and greenery, the cliffs of Negril are one of Jamaica's foremost tourist attractions.*

89 *The lush vegetation ever-present in Jamaica appears to lay seige to the tiny bay of Navy Island, just off Port Antonio.*

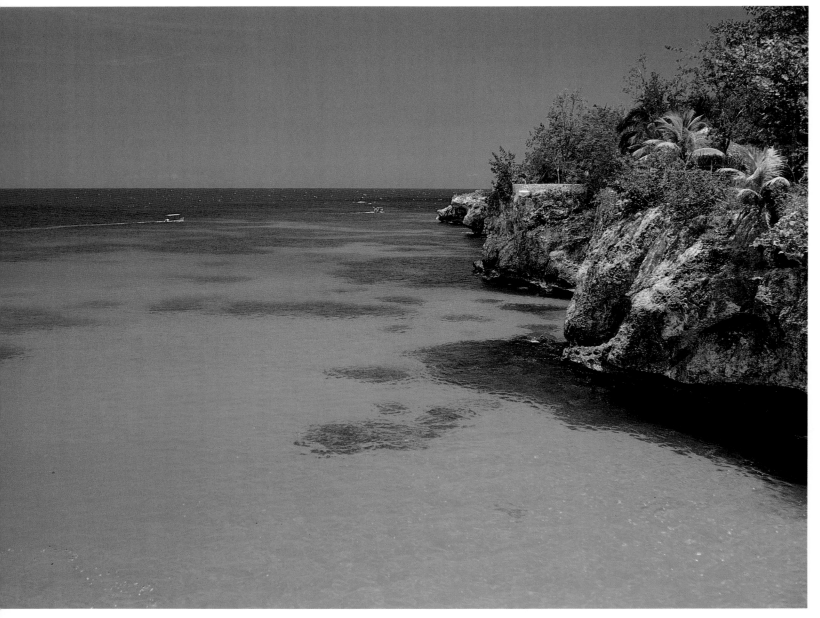

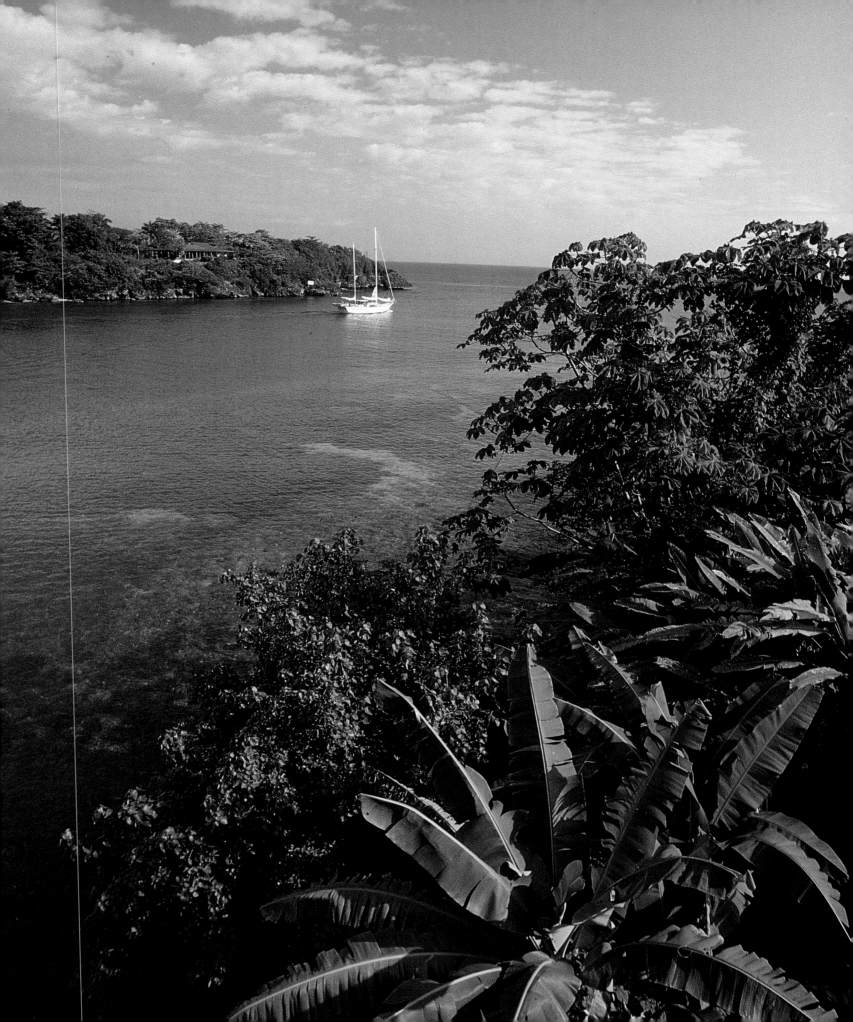

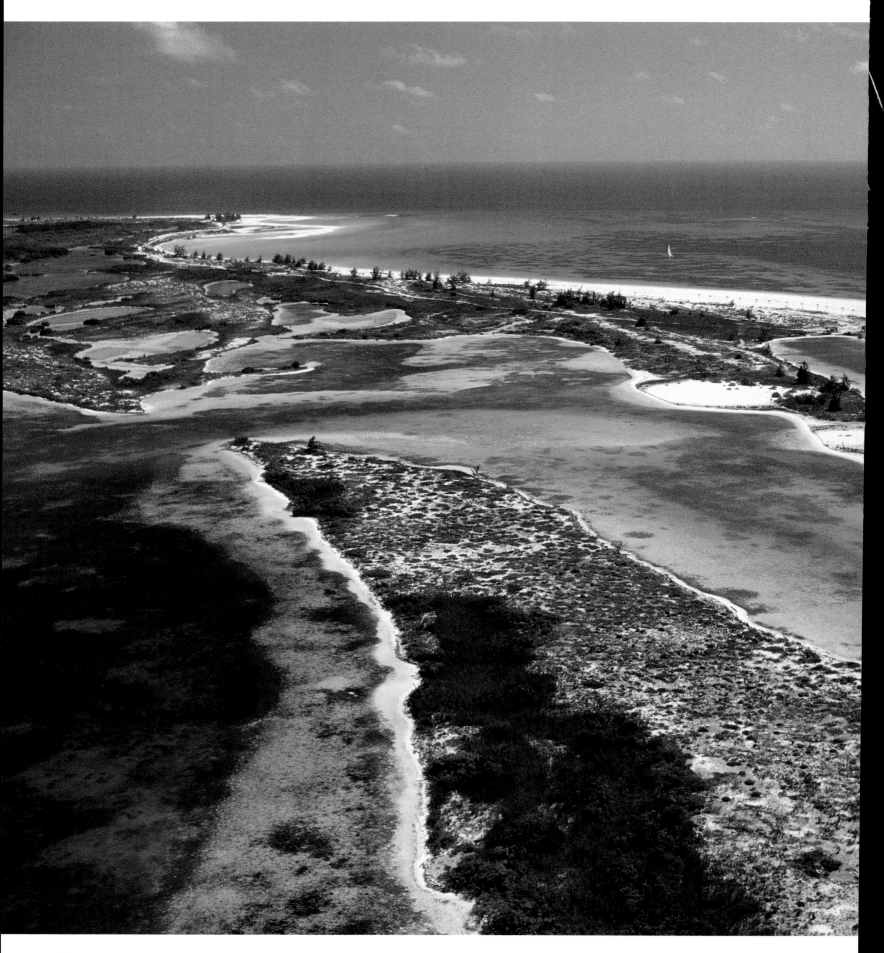

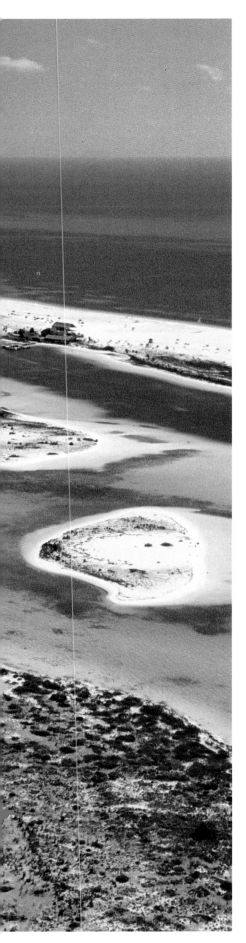

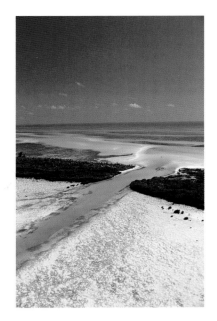

90-91  *Cays are small low islets of coral sand, typically found in the tropical seas of the Caribbean; around the coast of Cuba there are more than 350.*

91 top  *Coral beaches, crystal-clear waters and seabeds teeming with life: Cayo Largo epitomizes the natural splendour of the Caribbean.*

91 centre and bottom  *Cayo Largo is a stunning stretch of sand, 19 miles long and 7 miles wide. With its dazzling colours and enormous variety of underwater flora and fauna, it rivals even the most celebrated coral reefs.*

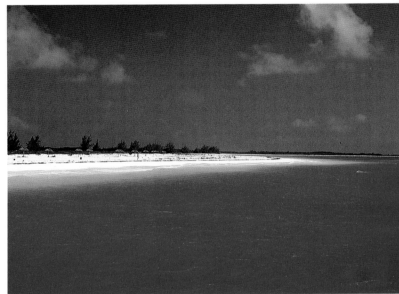

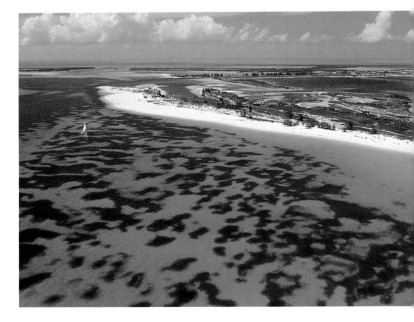

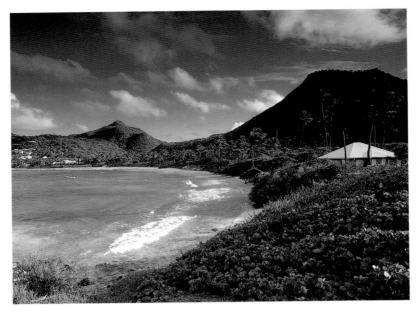

92 top *The picturesque bays of St.Barthélemy are frequented by chic, well-heeled tourists; the secluded setting and crystal-clear water of Anses de Lorient makes it one of the most popular on the island.*

92 bottom *The short runway of St.Barthélemy's tiny airport has not spoilt the enchanting picture presented by Anse de St.Jean, with its unbelievably blue sea.*

93 *Possibly the longest and most famous beach of St.Barthélemy is Anse des Flamands, a never-crowded strip of fine-grained sand, sheltered from wind and breakers.*

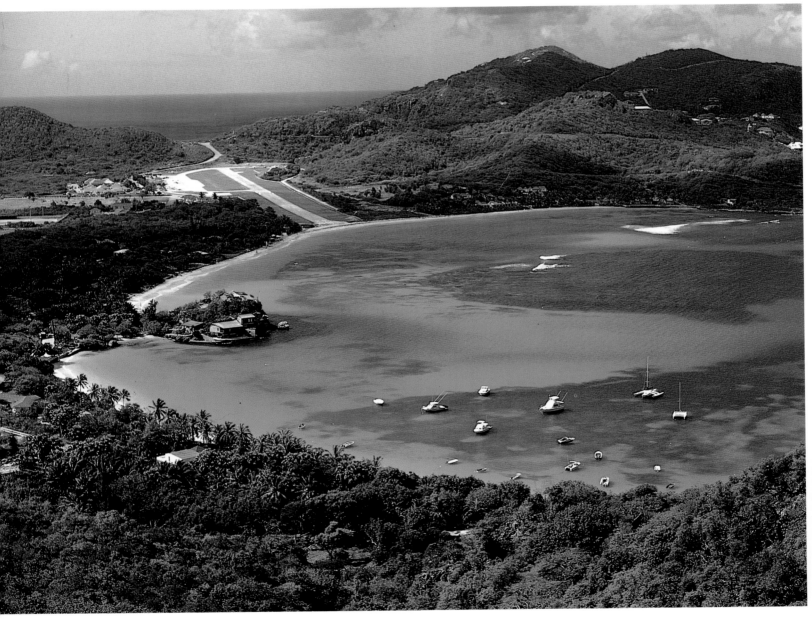

94-95 *Anses de Lorient is surely one of St.Barthélemy's loveliest beaches. St.Barts, as the island is called by its inhabitants, was first settled by the French and then leased to the Swedes in 1785 for about a century; Breton and Norman dialects are still spoken in a few of its villages, a reminder of the island's variegated past.*

96-97 *Anse des Flamands is considered by many to be one of the most beautiful beaches in the world: its protected position ensures that this long stretch of fine white sand is never troubled by the winds and occasional storms that sweep across the island of St.Barthélemy.*

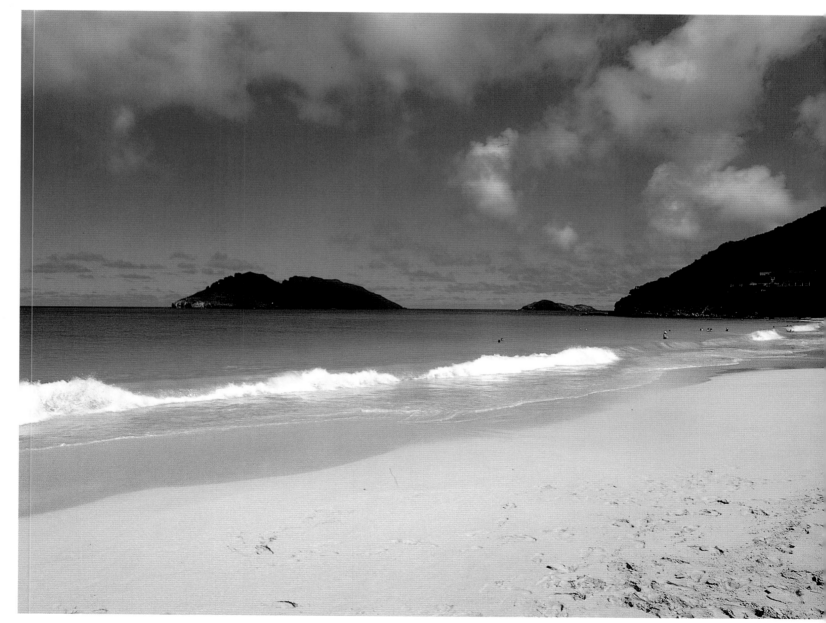

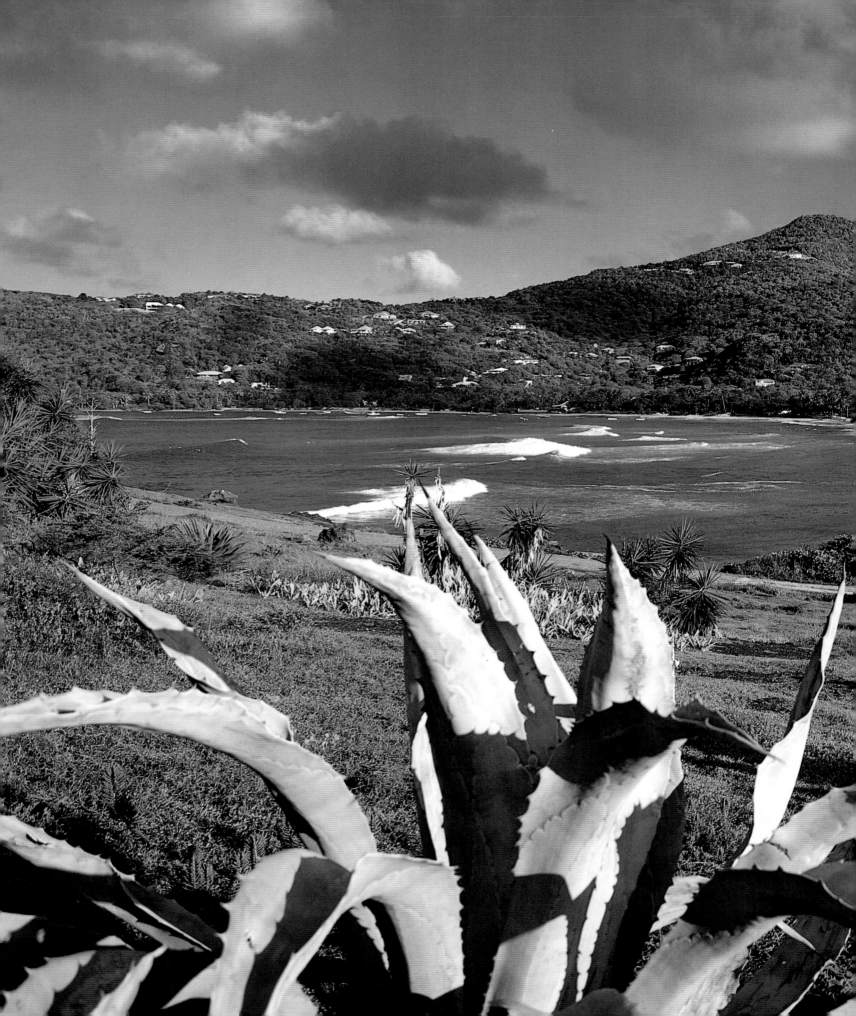

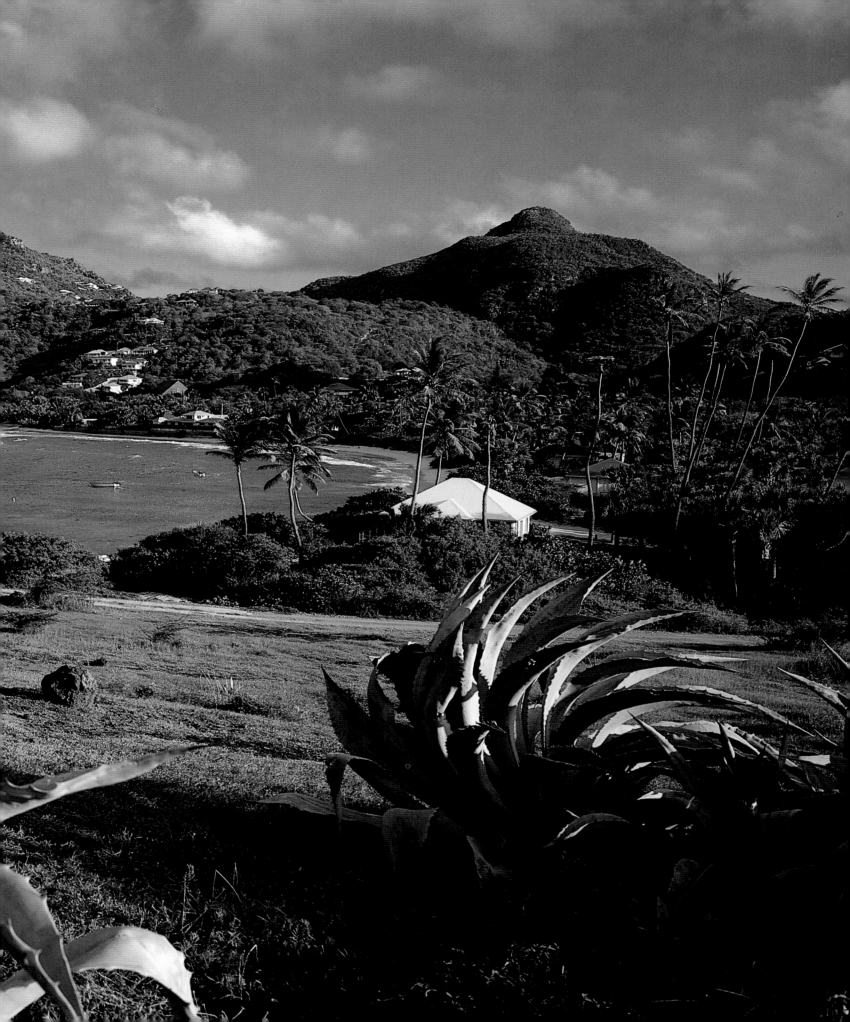

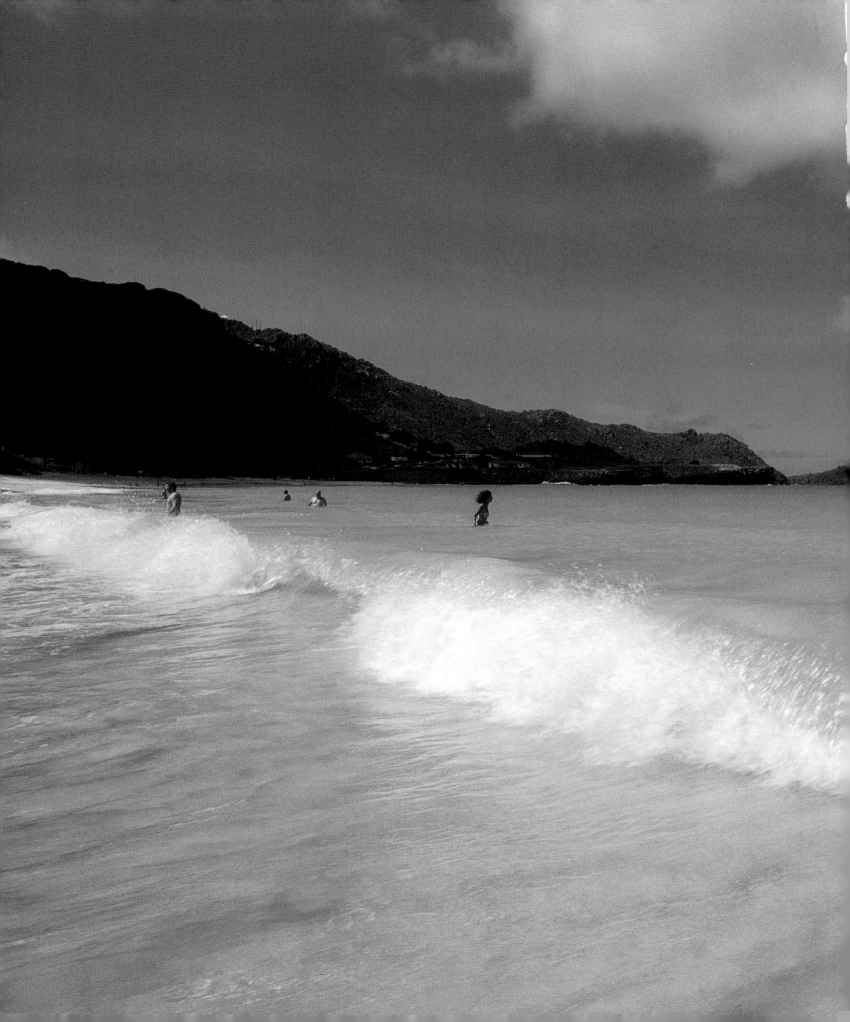

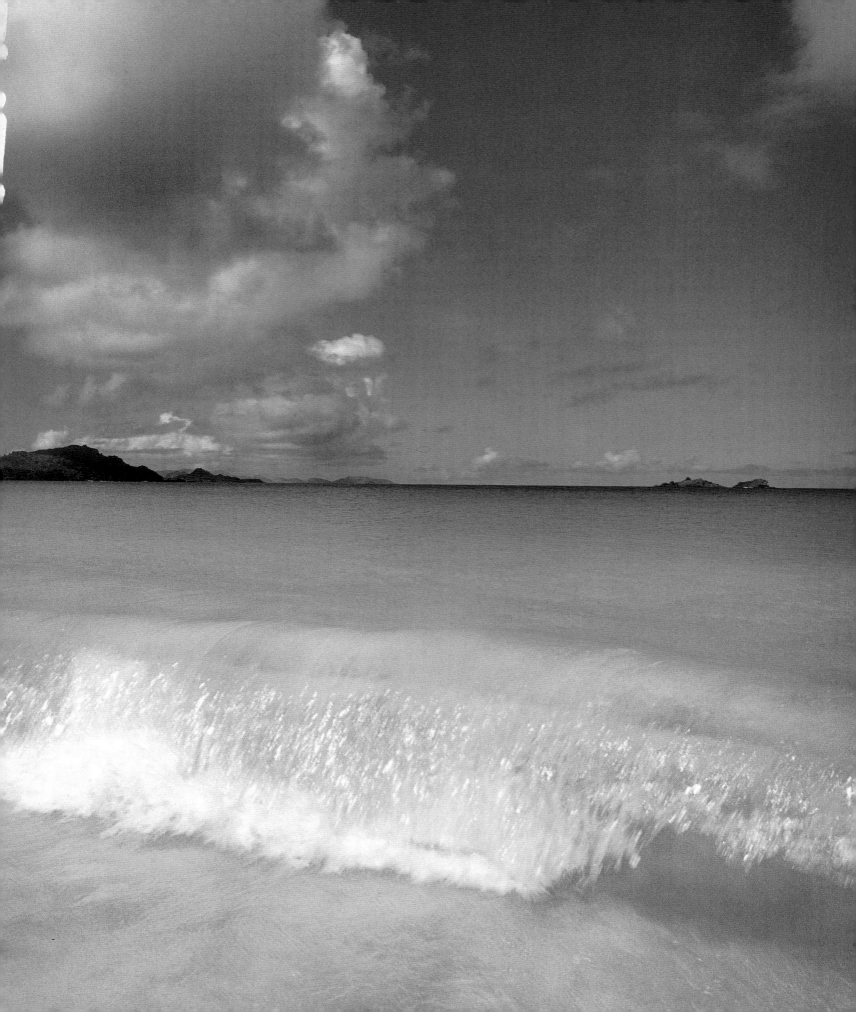

# The islands of the capricious giant

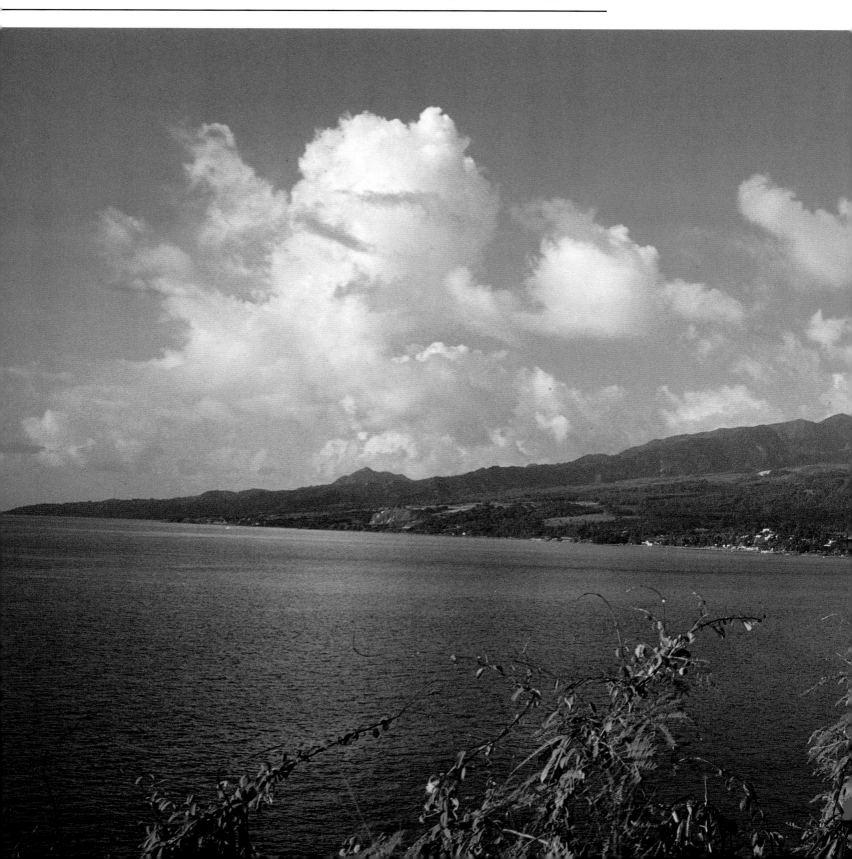

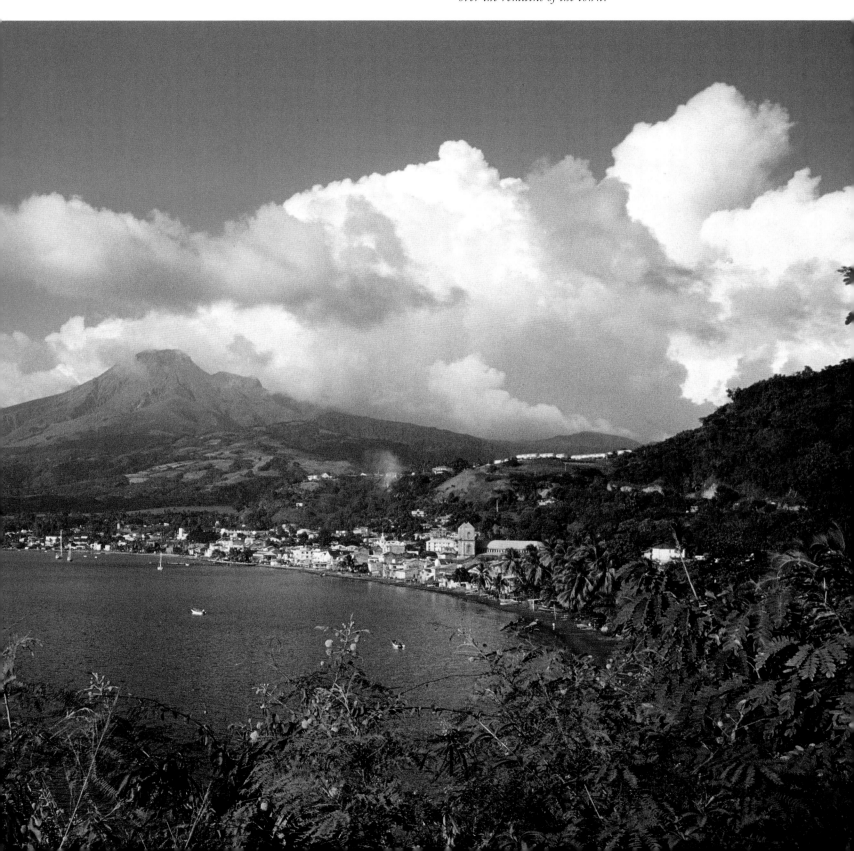

98-99  *On the west coast of Martinique, north of Fort-de-France, is St.Pierre, former main town of the island; it was destroyed by lava erupting from Montagne Pelée, the capricious, still-active volcano which towers threateningly over the remains of the town.*

# Crystal-clear waters

**100-101** *Lapped by the deep blue-green ocean, the beach and bay of Marigot are the foremost attractions of the capital town of the French half of the island of St.Martin. Major contributions to the picturesque scene are made by Fort St.Louis, with its superb panorama of the bay, and the tourist marina which attracts hundreds of the finest boats in the Caribbean.*

**102-103** *Nearly touching in Antigua are a freshwater lake and the ocean. Antigua is famed for its many beaches; though they have never been counted, the local people are convinced there are 365, one for every day of the year.*

**104-105** *Brown-sand beaches and gently rolling hills thick with vegetation are typical features of the coastline of Basse-Terre and unmistakable evidence of the island's volcanic origin.*

**106-107** *La Pointe des Chateaux is a long tongue of land extending from the island of Grande-Terre towards the Atlantic and terminating in rugged, wind-swept cliffs.*

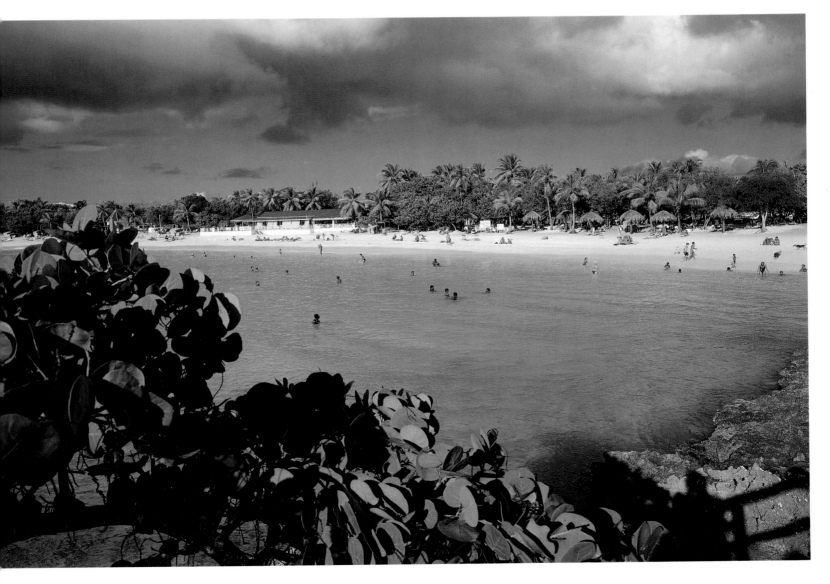

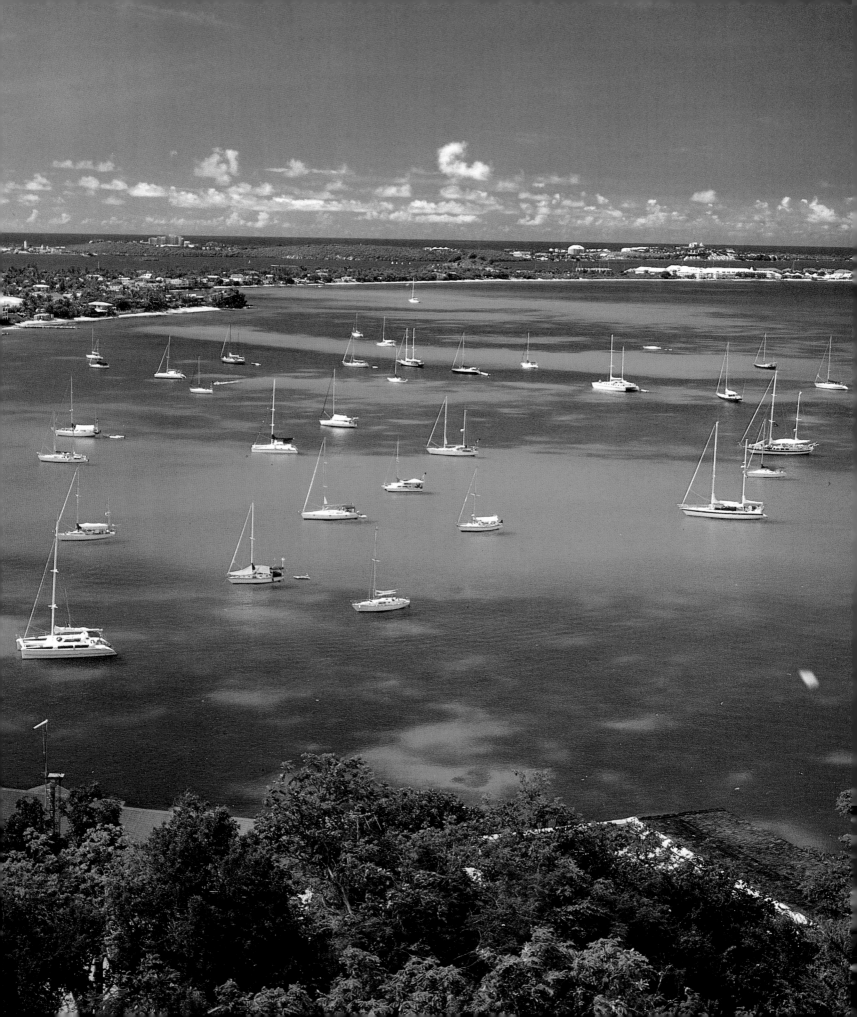

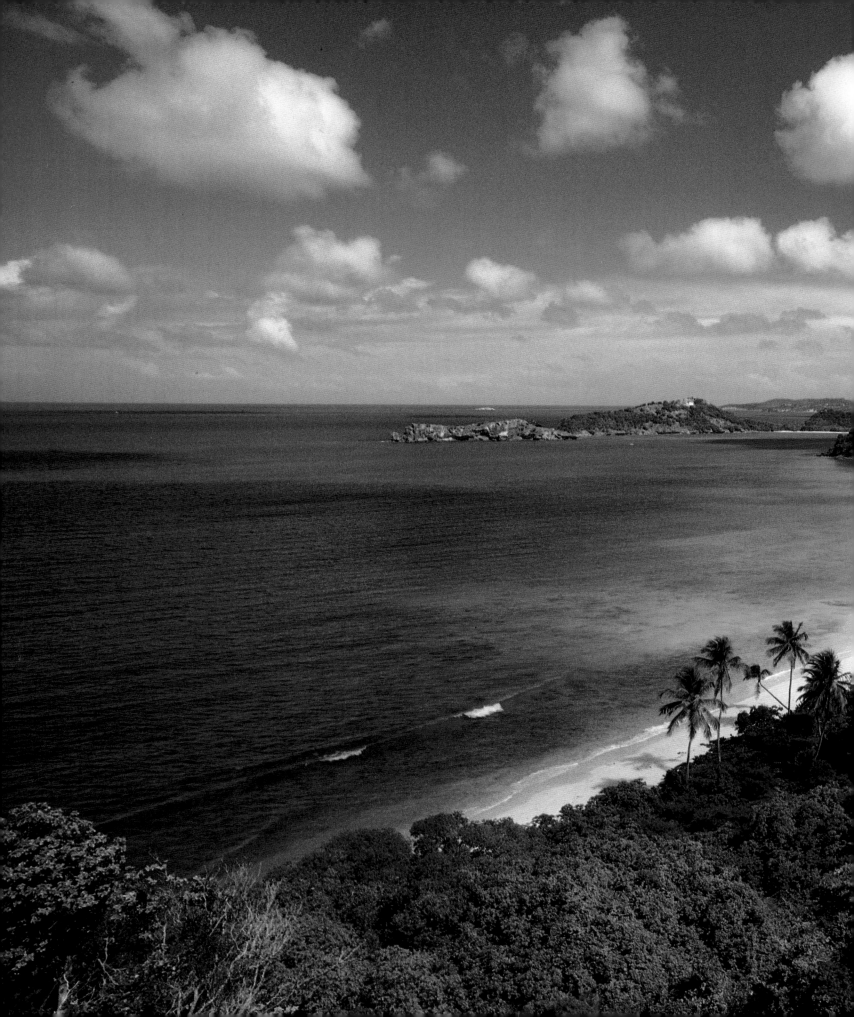

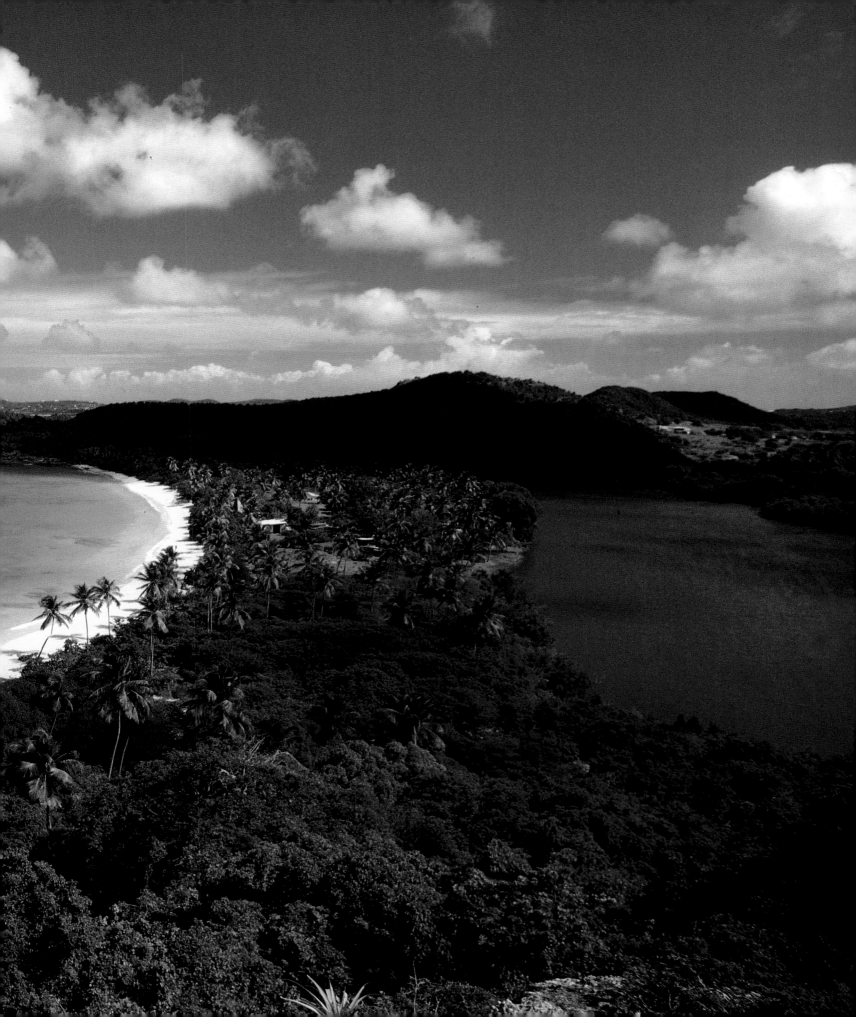

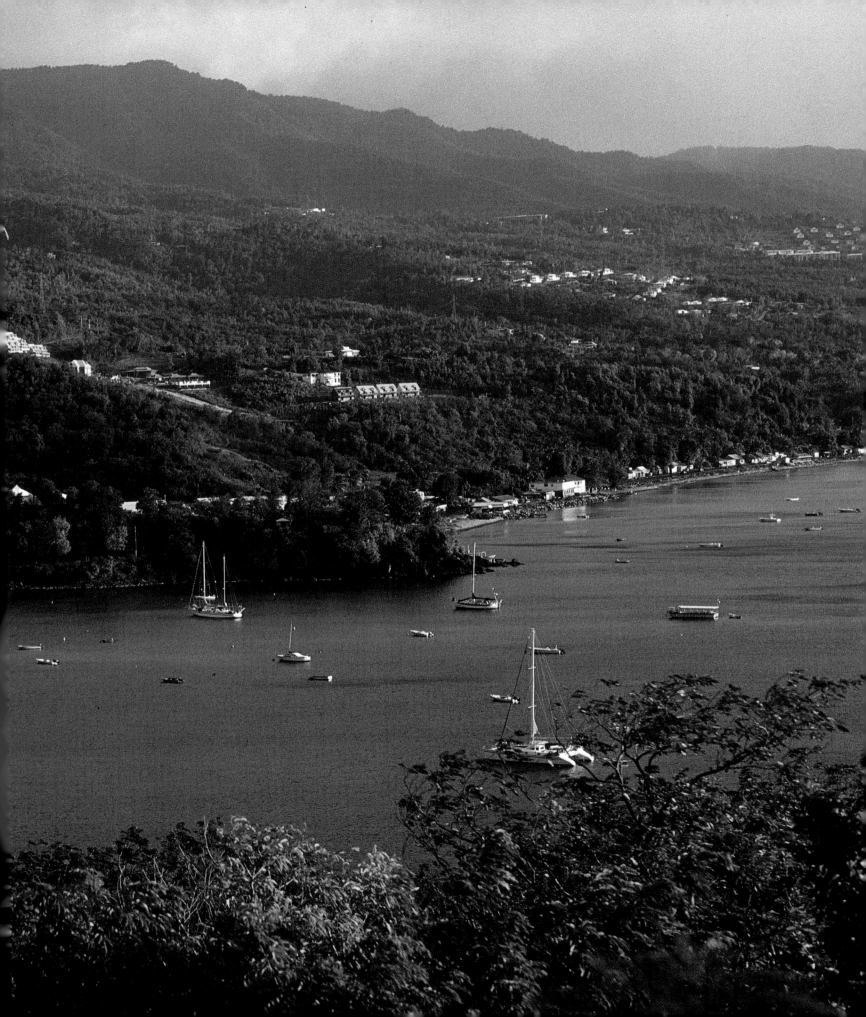

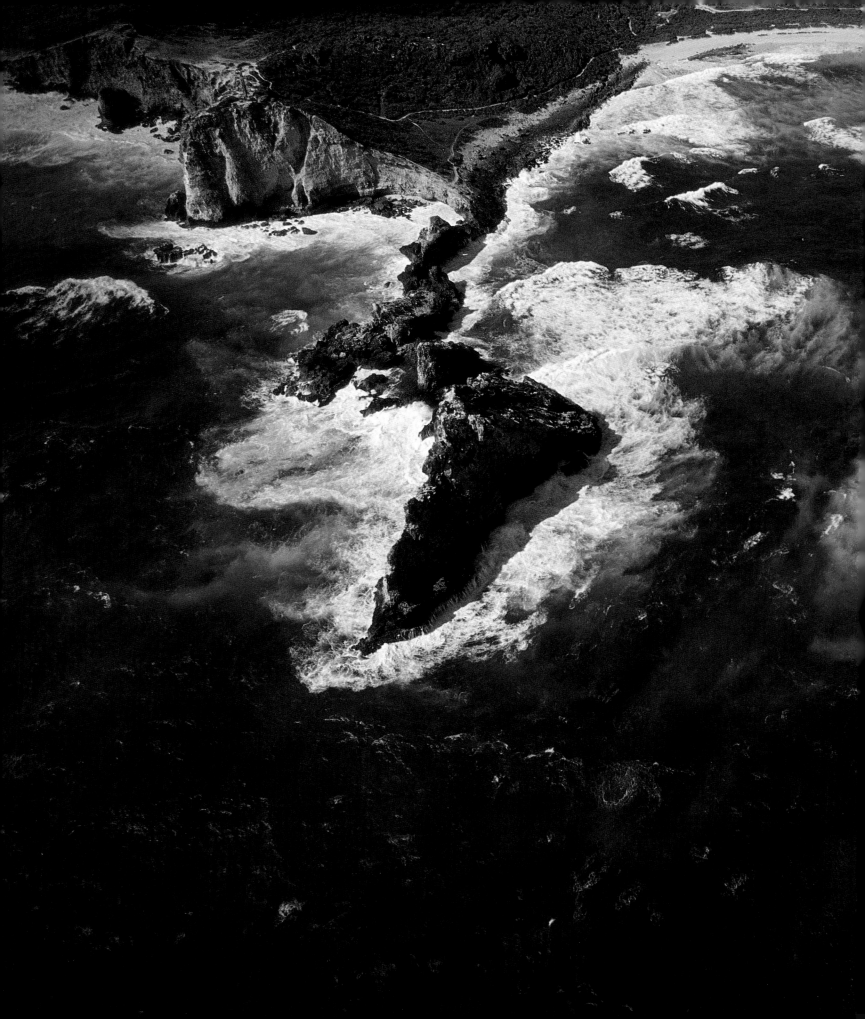

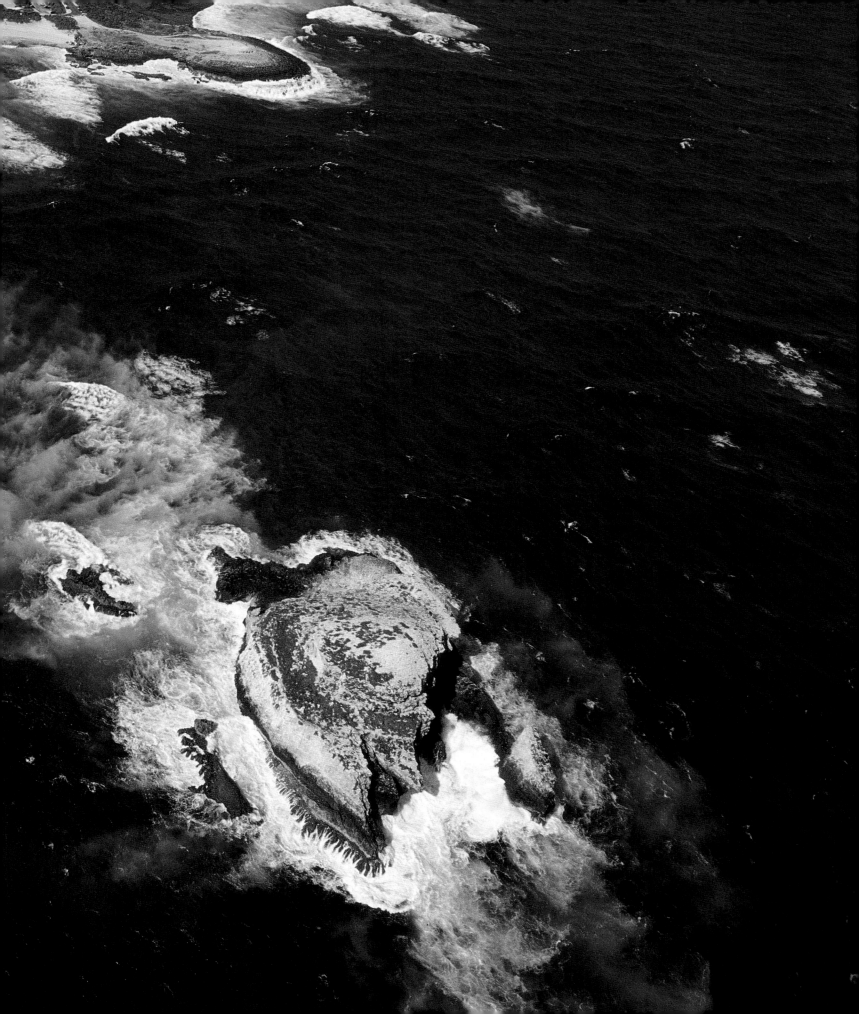

# Guadeloupe, the call of the rainforest

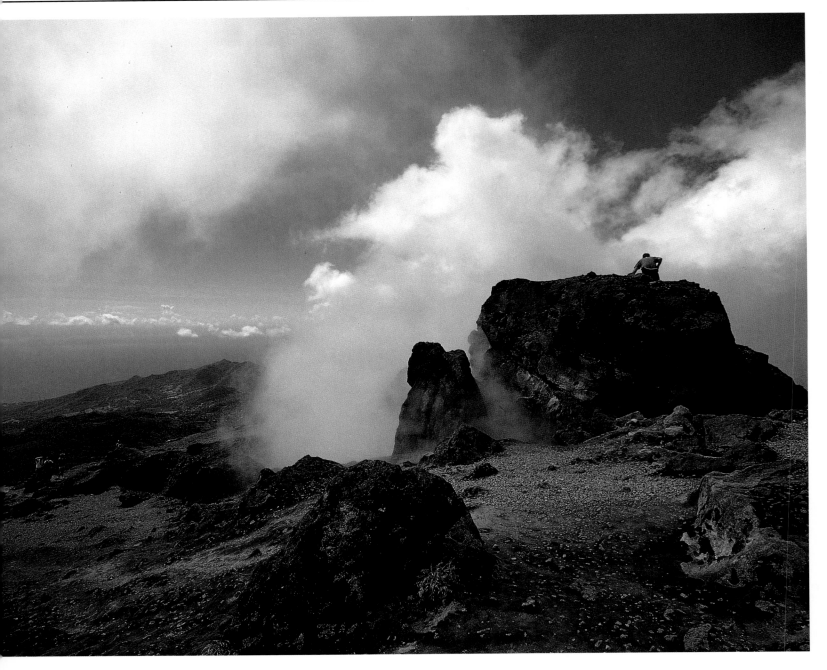

108  *High up in the heart of the Parc Naturel de Guadeloupe, columns of steam rise from the volcanic vents of Soufrière.*

109  *In the Parc Naturel de Guadeloupe the Chutes du Carbet are an impressive sight, plunging down through the impenetrable vegetation of the tropical rainforest.*

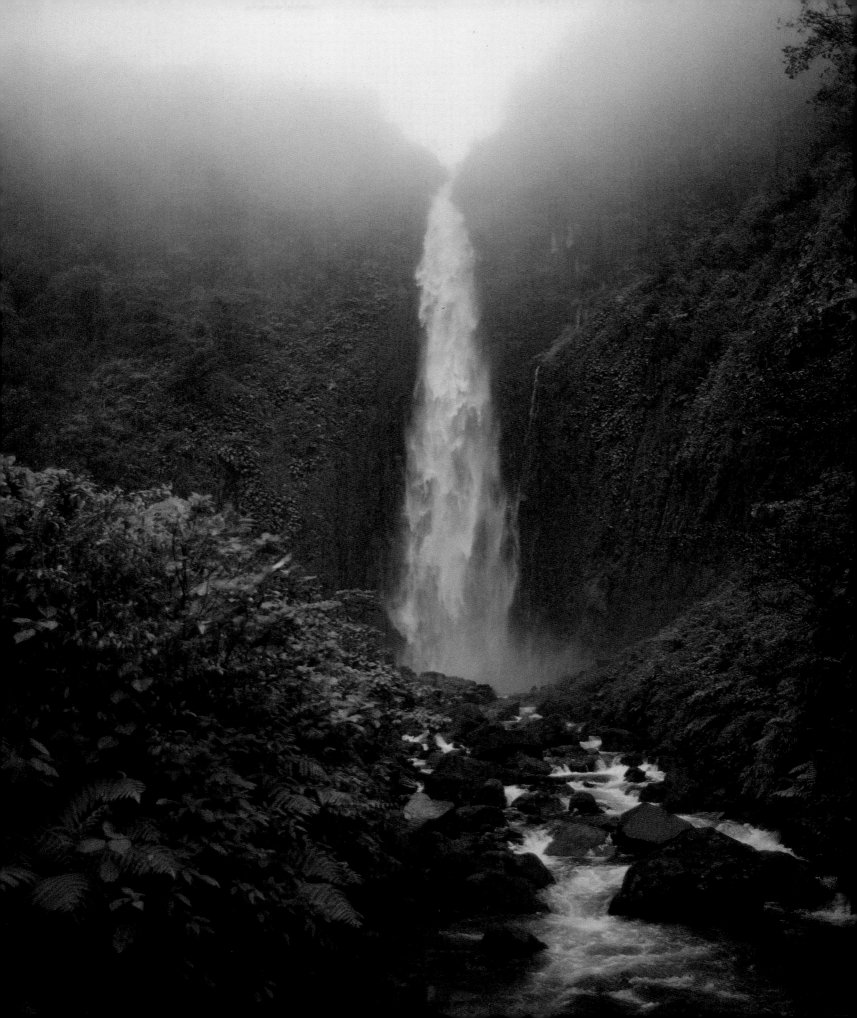

110-111   *The terrain in the interior of Guadeloupe is for the most part covered with luxuriant vegetation: dense tropical forests grow in the valleys and on the mountains, the mass of green occasionally briefly interrupted by the rushing water of torrents which force their way through the undergrowth.*

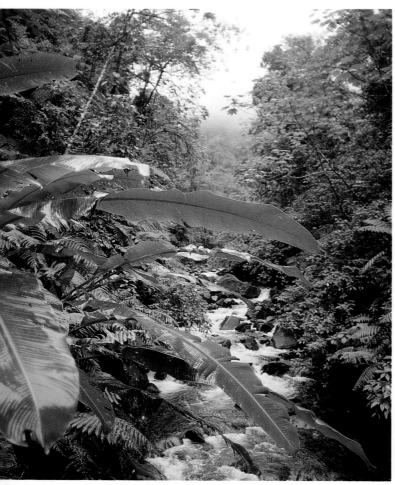

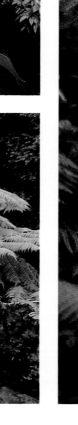

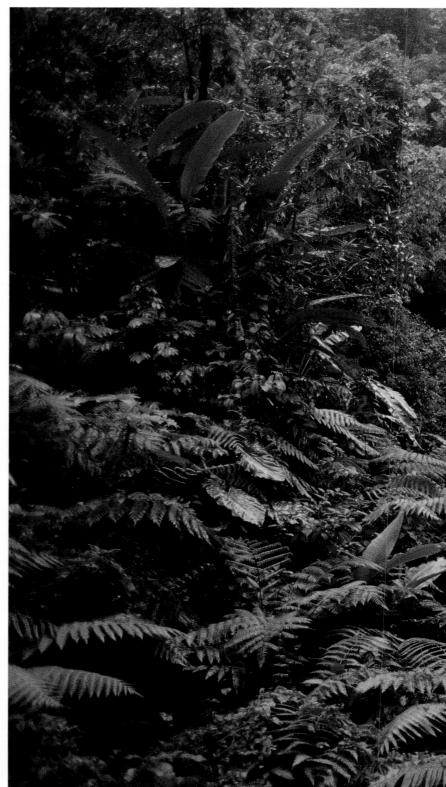

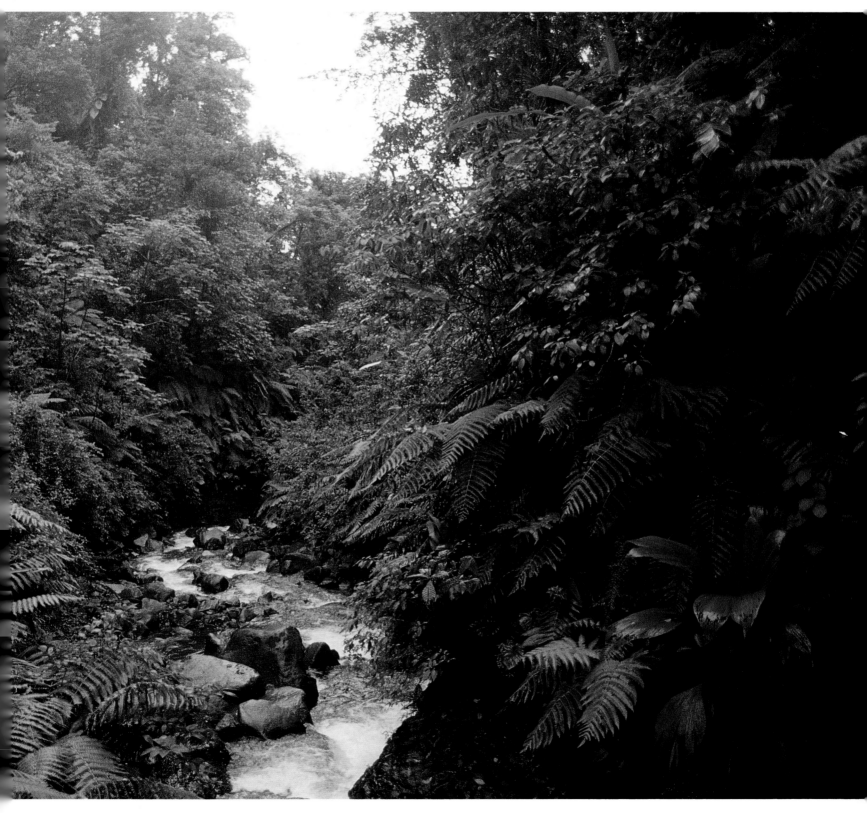

# The Virgin Islands,
# wonders of the Caribbean

112 and 113 top  *Renowned for its unspoilt beauty, the island of St.John is practically a natural park, undeveloped and undisturbed: much of its territory is part of the Virgin Islands National Park.*

113 bottom  *A catamaran flying the American flag has beached on the smooth sand of Buck Island, one of the gems of the US Virgin Islands.*

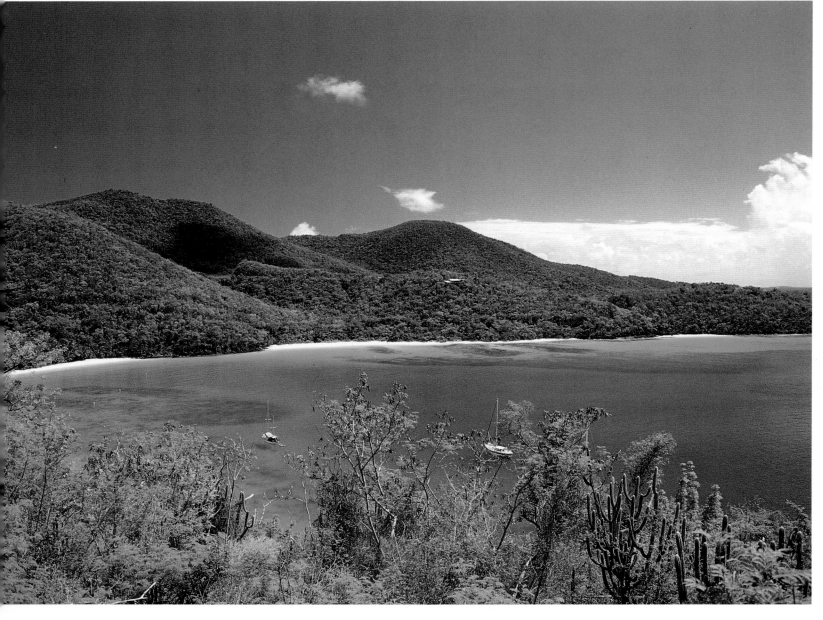

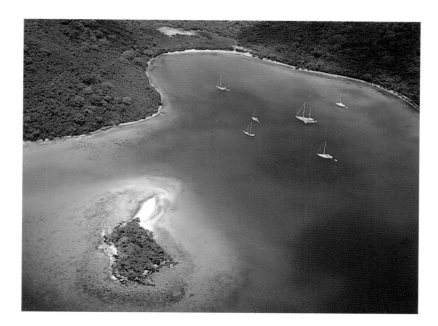

114-115 *A narrow strip of amazingly white sand stands its own against the encroaching tropical vegetation: this enchanting place is Trunk Bay on St. John, the most virgin of the US Virgin Islands. It is generally considered the loveliest beach on St. John, favoured by scuba enthusiasts as a departure point for stunning dives.*

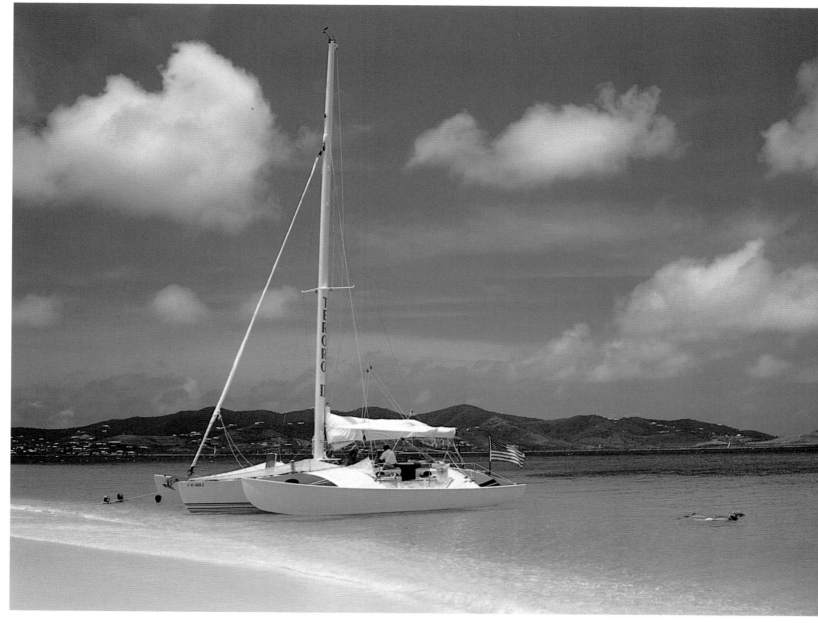

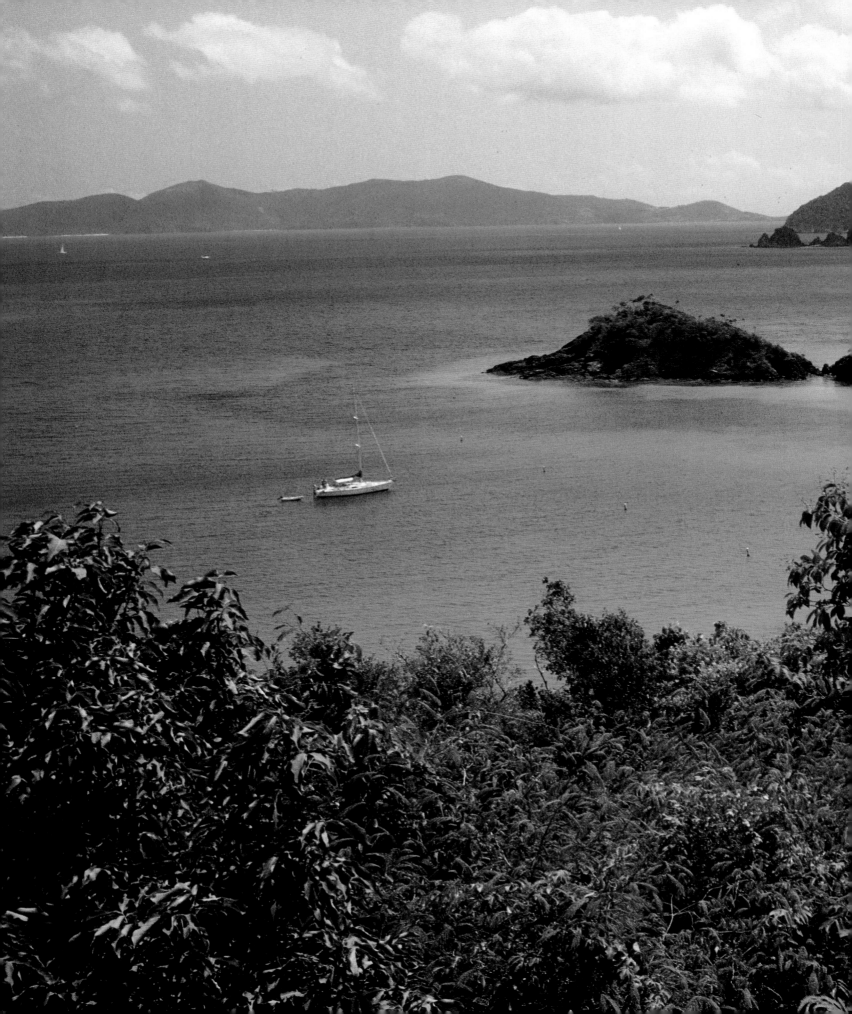

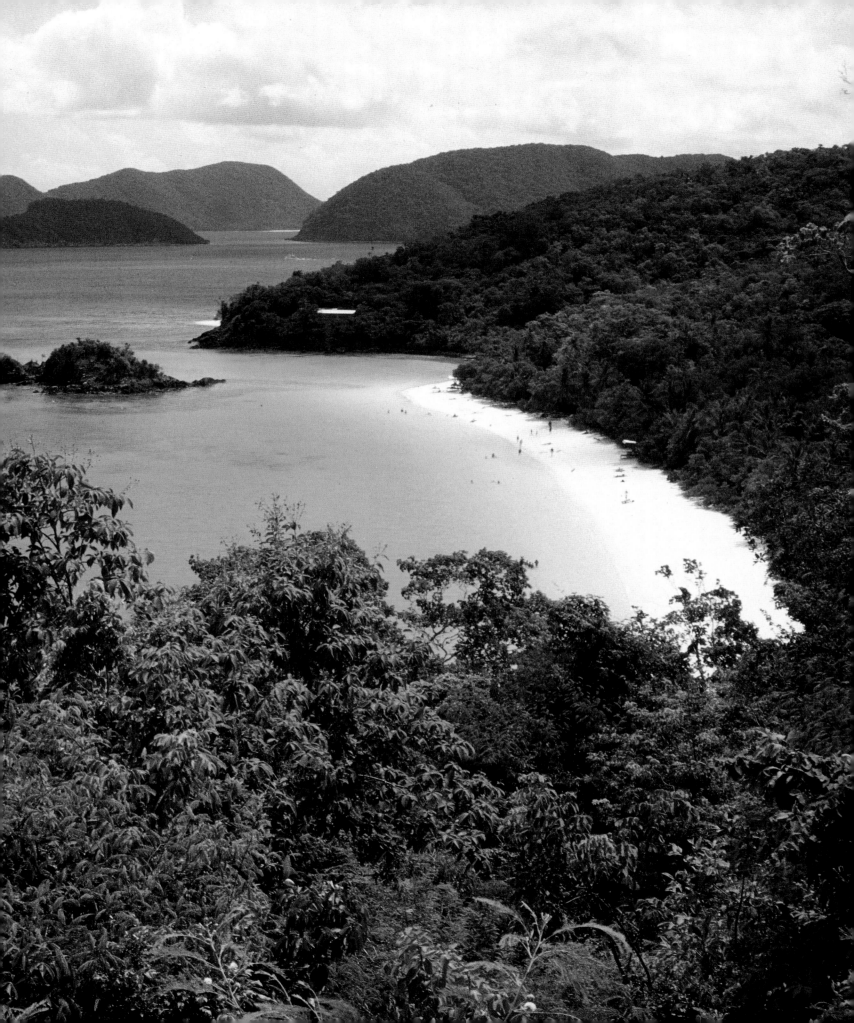

# St. Lucia, home of the twin volcanoes

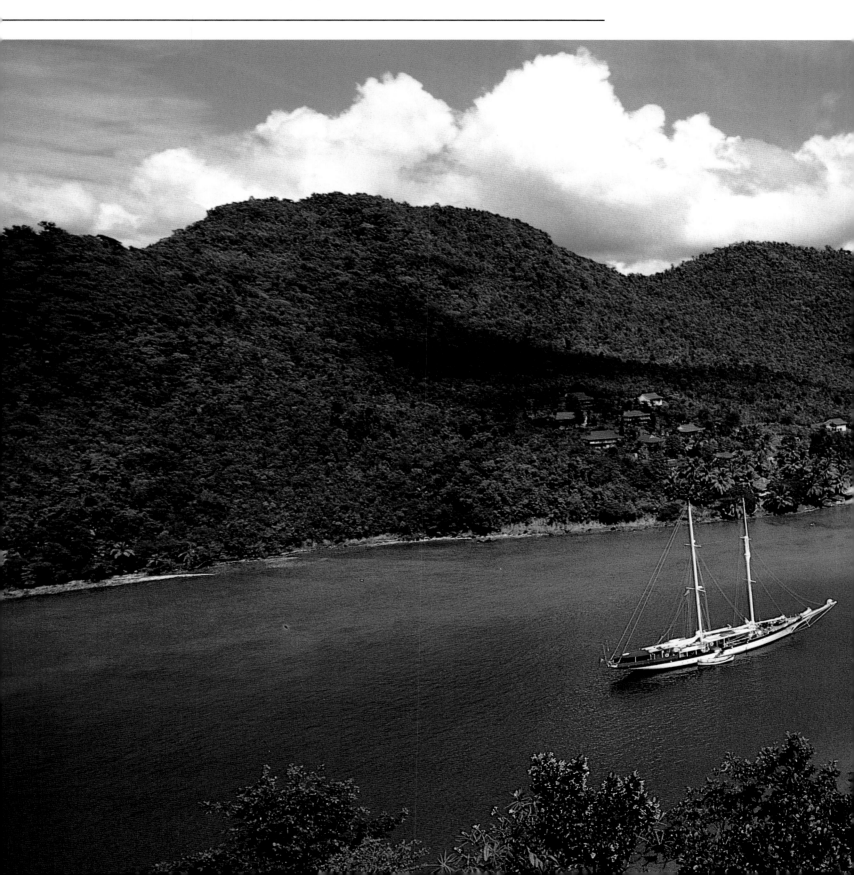

116-117  *On the west coast of the island of St.Lucia, where it is rivalled only by Castries and Rodney Bay, Marigot Bay is one of the most fascinating bays of the Caribbean; its small but well equipped harbour is busy with tourist boats all year round.*

118-119  *Prominent against the horizon, like two pitiless deities, are the green peaks of the twin volcanoes, Gros Piton and Petit Piton: soaring from the sea to a height of 2,300 feet, their shapely forms are a distinctive landmark on St.Lucia.*

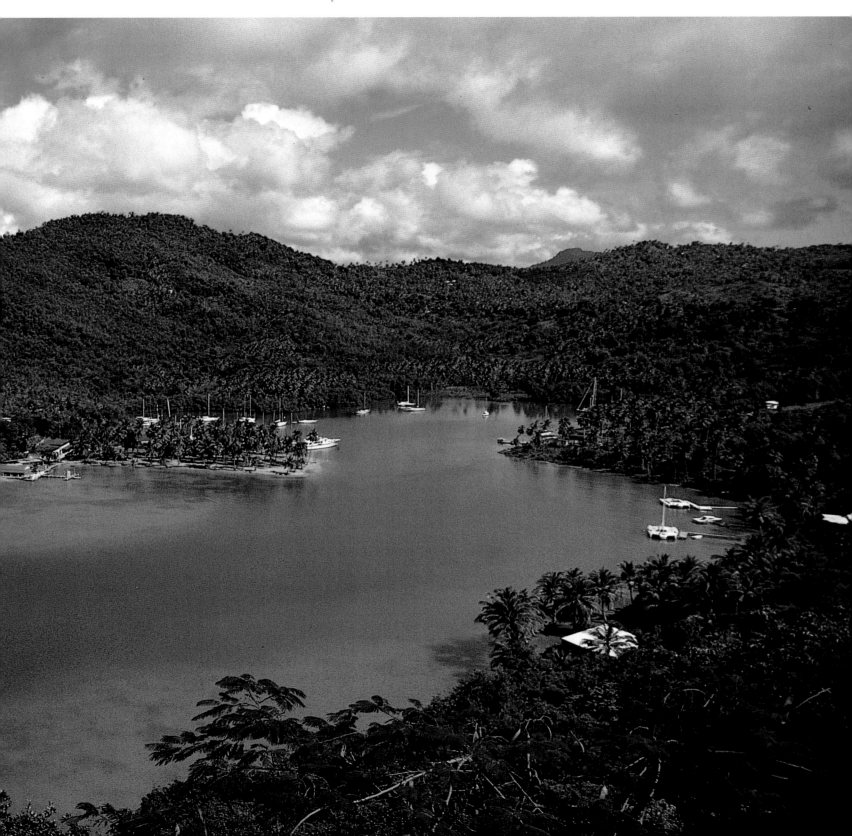

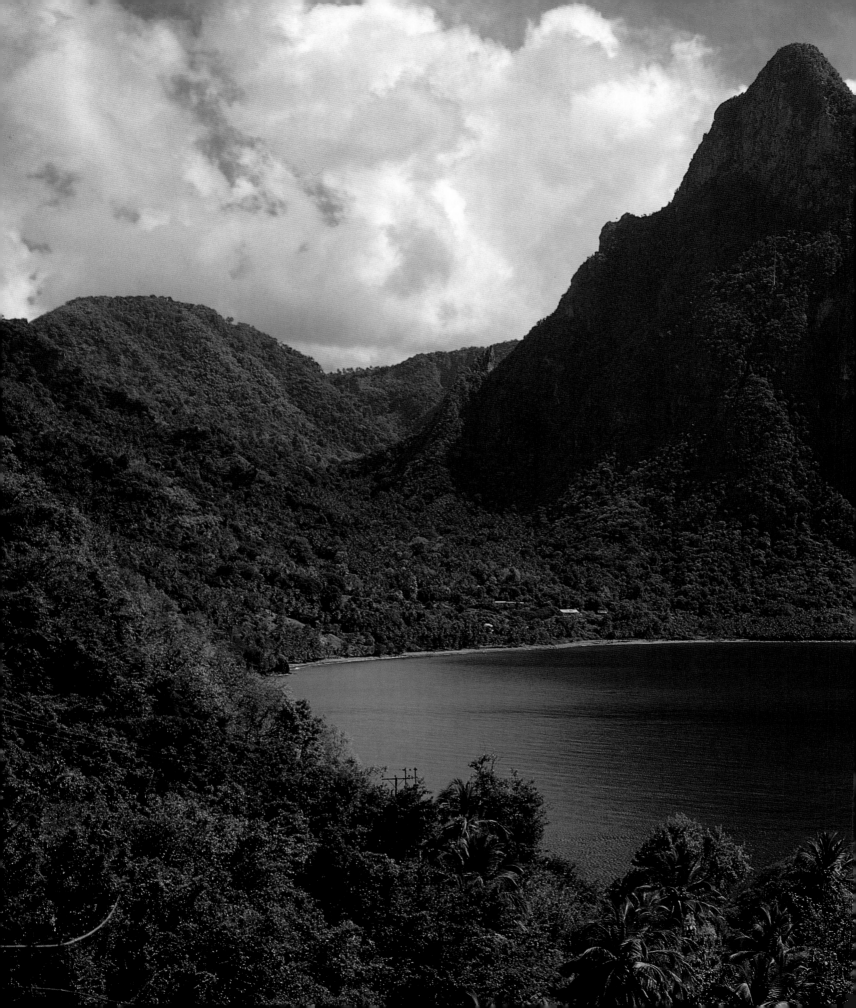

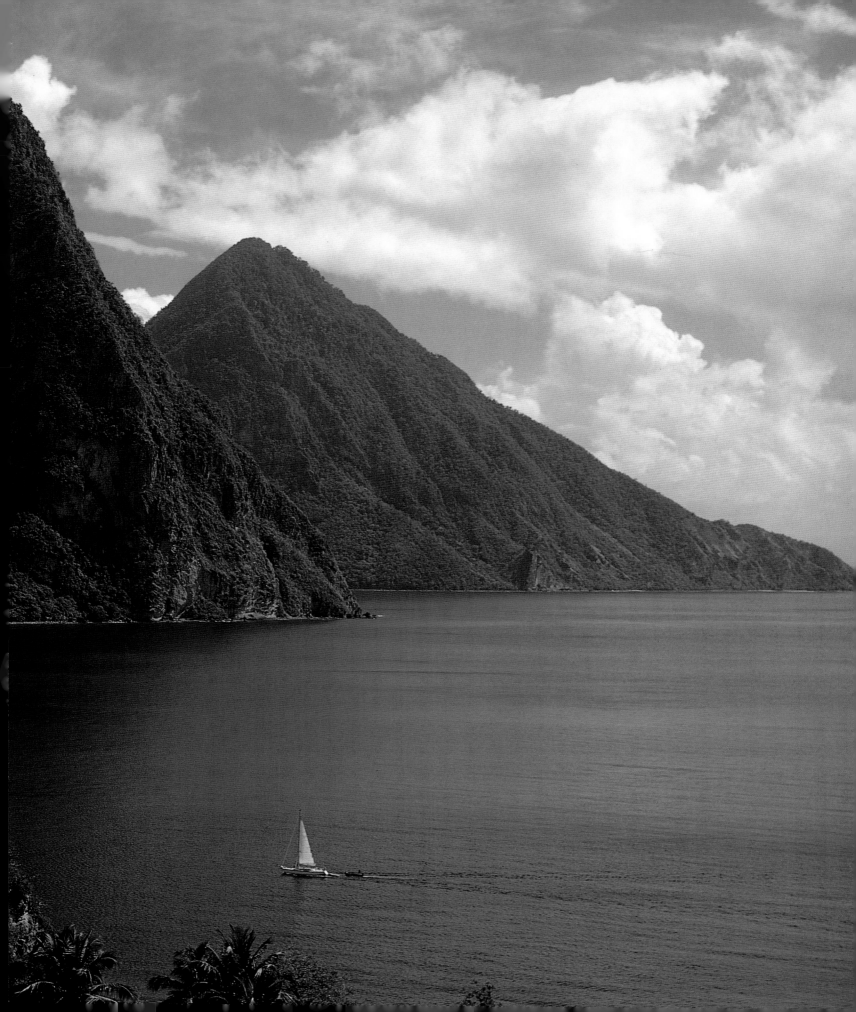

# Land of corals

120  *The hundred or so islands and cays that make up the archipelago of the Grenadines, scattered between Grenada and St. Vincent, offer an idyllic setting for sailing and underwater fishing.*

121  *Every shade of blue and green can be seen blended in the warm waters around the tiny island of Petit Tabac, in the Grenadines.*

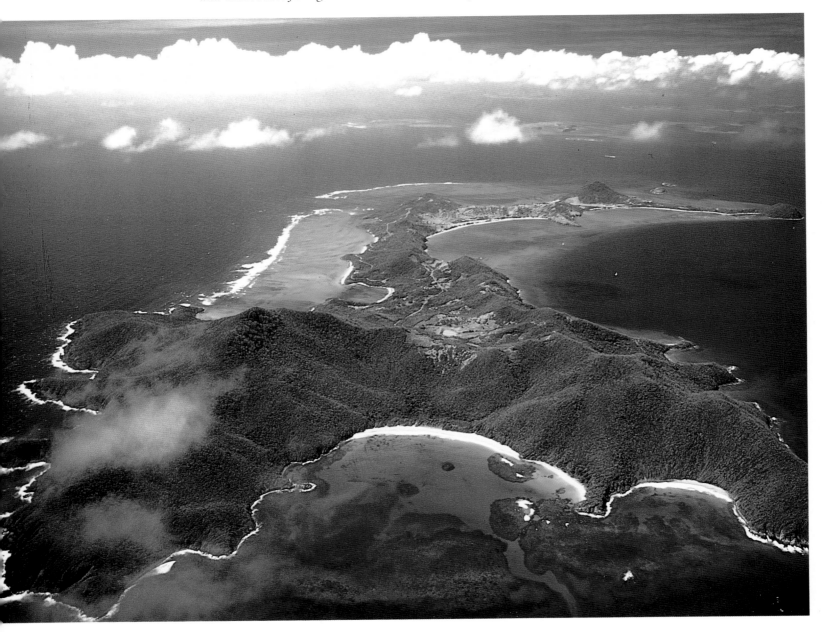

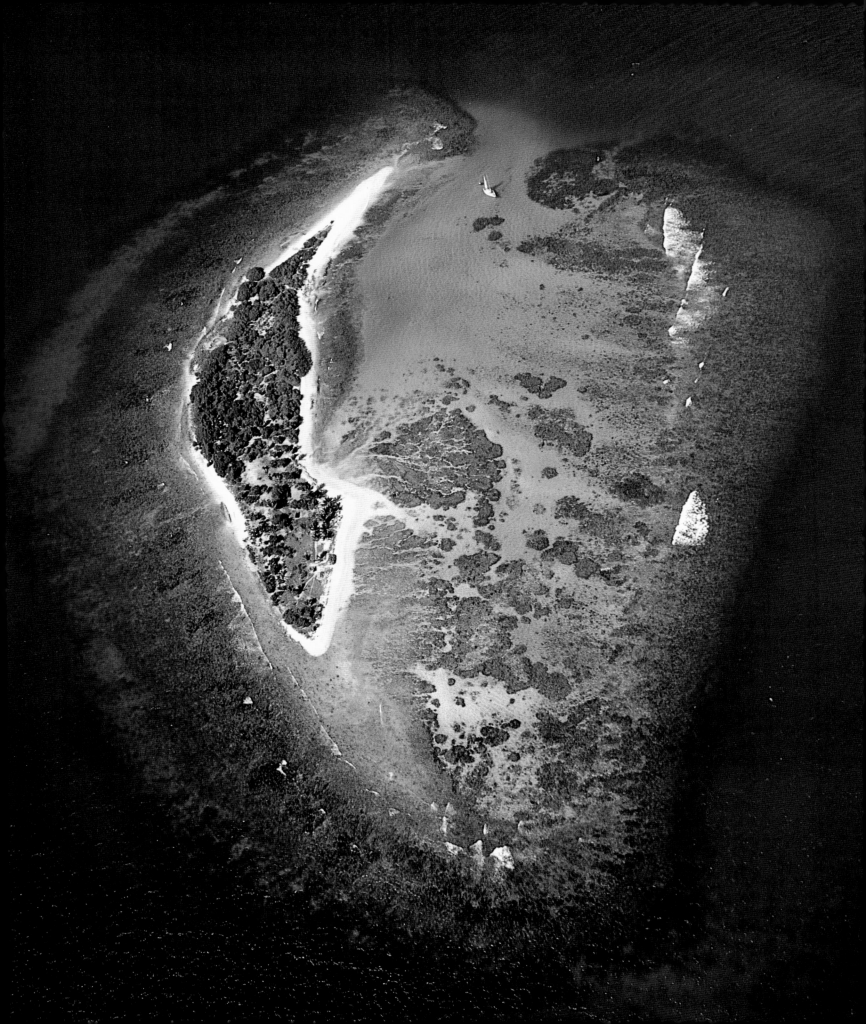

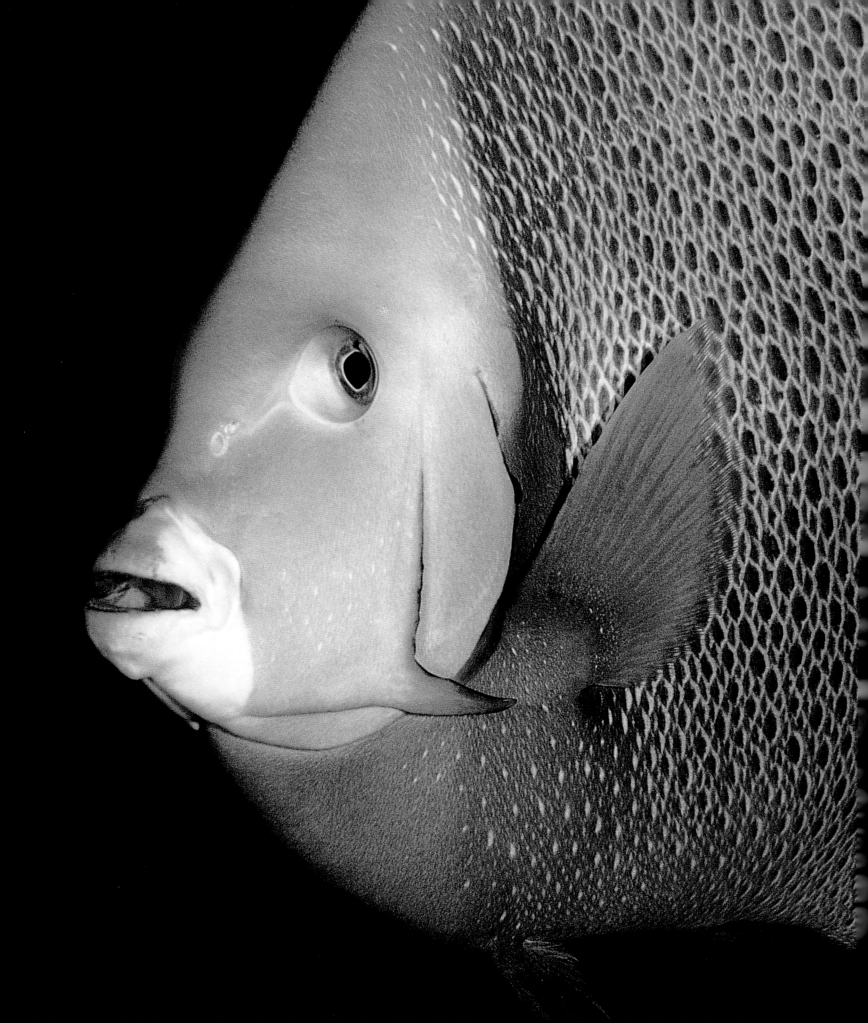

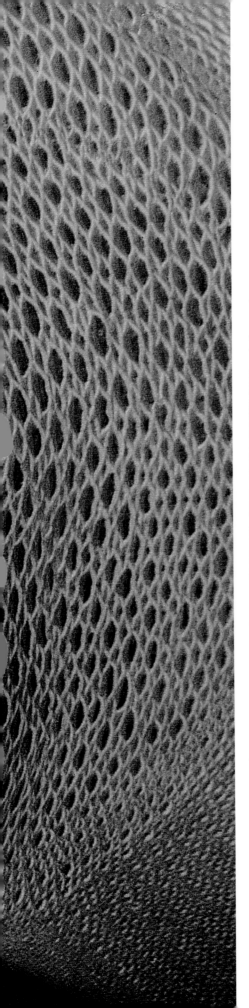

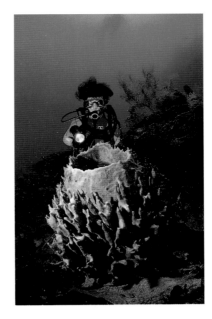

122 *Countless species of fish populate the Caribbean Sea and the underwater world of the Tropics holds constant surprises for divers: for instance, encounters with angelfish, like the one shown here.*

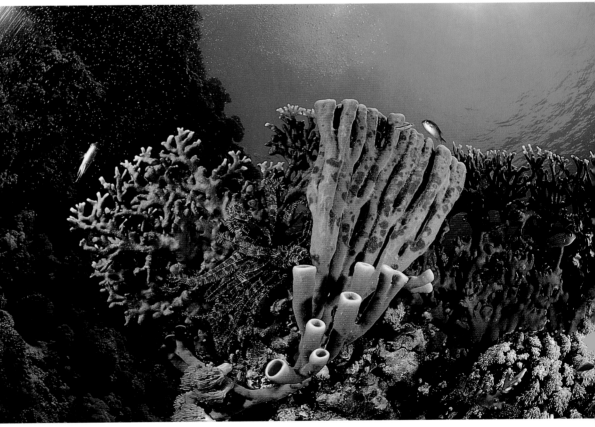

123 top *All kinds of life forms exist on the floor of the Caribbean, their breeding and growth encouraged by favourable currents; pictured in this photo is a gigantic sponge, of dimensions not infrequently seen in these waters.*

123 bottom *For some creatures, living on a tropical coral reef can mean a constant struggle to survive: here a branching sponge fights for living space with two "bushes" of fire-red coral.*

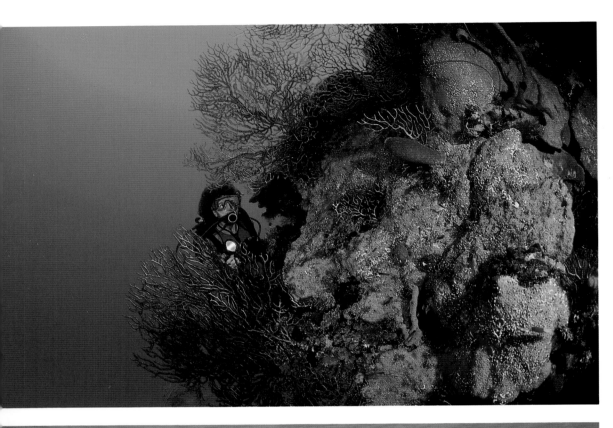

124 top *A colony of deep red corals has taken root on the wall of a reef: for scuba divers there are many stunningly beautiful sights on the bed of the Caribbean.*

124 bottom *Long-snouted dolphins (Stenidae) are among the most playful of all the sea mammals: in the waters of the Caribbean it is not unusual to come across these gregarious creatures, swimming alone or in groups; in either case they appear to enjoy the company of divers.*

125 *Shoals of spotted and blue-striped fish swim close to a huge coral fan, in search of food. The exceptionally bright Caribbean light and the shallow water around many of the coral reefs make visibility below the surface excellent and divers can take splendid photos.*

126-127 *The scenery offered on the east of Barbados is a mix of stunning beaches and stretches of rocky cliffs swept by winds off the Atlantic. Compared with more tranquil Caribbean shores beauty here has a wilder dimension: breakers crashing on rocks at high tide, winds bending the tall palm trees and a prevailing impression of being in contact with the more authentic side of nature.*

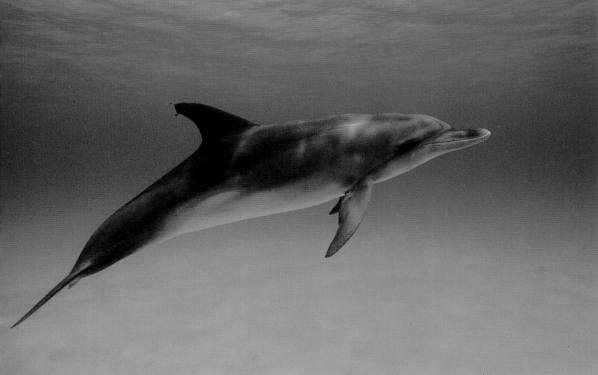

128 *The colours of the setting sun light up Dickenson Bay, one of the "365 beaches" that the islanders of Antigua love to lay claim to. It vies with Runway Bay as the resort offering the finest tourist amenities on the whole island of Antigua.*

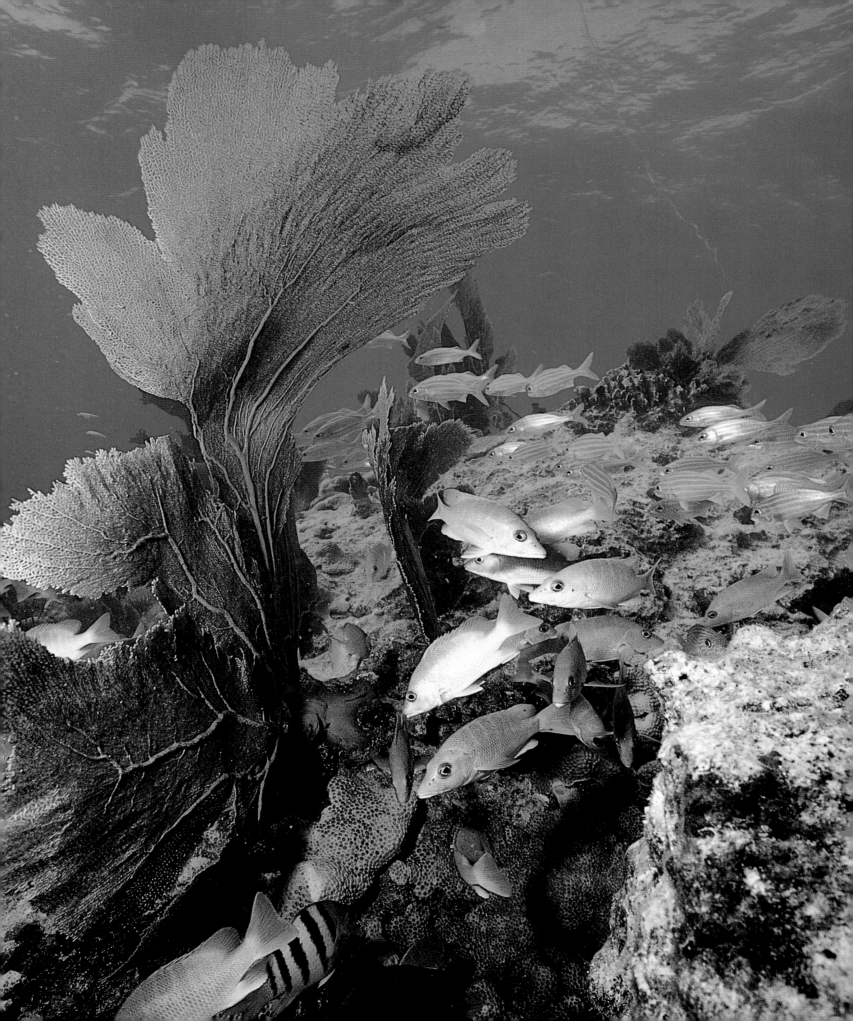

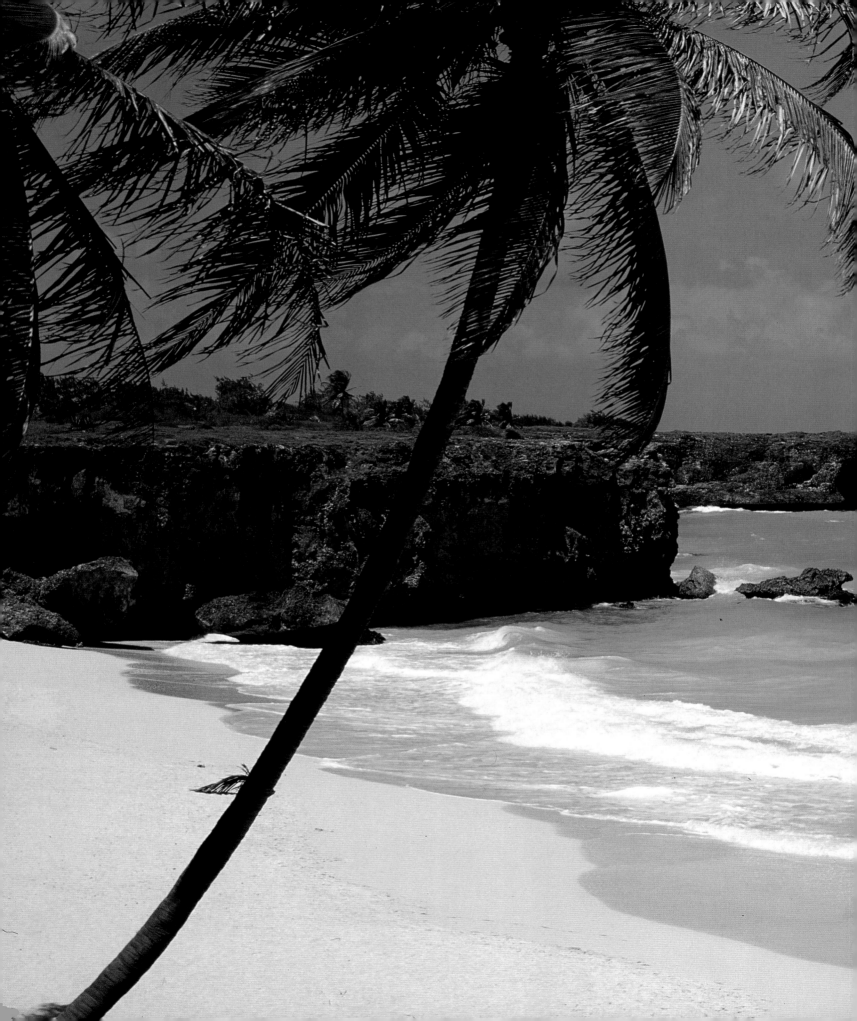

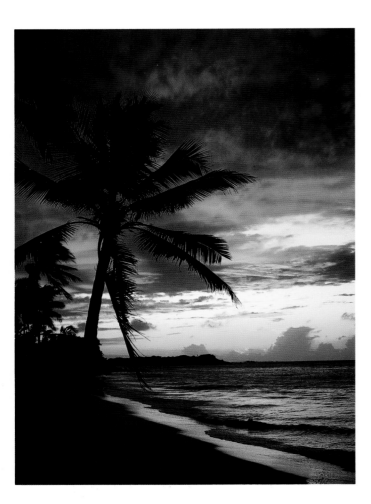

Photo Credits:

Marcello Bertinetti / White Star:
pages 8, 20-21, 43 top, 44-45, 54
bottom, 60 bottom, 62, 63, 80
bottom, 104-105, 106-107, 109,
110, 111.

Stefano Amantini / Atlantide:
pages 26-27, 42, 64-65, 67, 72, 73,
74, 75, 76, 77, 80 top, 81, 98-99,
108.

Atlantide / Bruce Coleman:
page 28 top.

Alastair Balck / Overseas:
page 116-117.

Cotton Coulson / Stock House:
page 120.

Bob Cranston / Panda Photo:
page 124 bottom.

Guido Cozzi / Atlantide:
backcover, pages 6-7, 46-47, 68-69,
70-71, 89, 92 top, 93, 94-95, 96-97,
100, 101.

Fausto Giaccone / SIE:
page 39 top.

Granata Press Service / Stock Image:
pages 57, 126-127.

Sylvain Grandadam / Stock House:
page 54 top.

Guillotean / Express / Grazia Neri:
page 102-103.

Chris Huxley / Planet Earth Pictures:
pages 12-13, 112, 121.

Alex Langley / Stoch House:
page 118-119.

M. Mastrorillo / SIE:
page 32-33.

Italo Monetti:
pages 14 top, 31 bottom, 35.

Mauro Parmesani and Patrizia
Miazzo:
pages 2-3, 15 bottom, 16-17, 29,
30-31, 31 centre, 34-35, 35 centre
left and centre right, 38-39, 39
bottom, 40 bottom, 83, 84-85,
86-87, 88, 90, 91.

Aldo Pavan:
pages 18-19, 35 top right, 35 bottom
right, 36-37.

Aldo Pearce / SIE:
page 28 bottom.

Andrea Pistolesi:
pages 43 bottom, 50-51, 52-53.

Photo Bank Singapore:
pages 9, 22-23, 24-25, 55, 78,
79, 128.

Davide Scagliola:
pages 66, 113, 114-115.

Lorenzo Sechi / SIE:
page 14.

Giovanni Simeone:
cover.

L. Sonnino Sorisio / Panda Photo:
page 60 top.

Steve Vidler / Stock House:
page 48-49.

Marco Stoppato:
page 82.

Angelo Tondini / Focus Team:
pages 40 top, 40-41, 56, 57, 58-59.

Michael Yamashita:
page 47.